P9-ECT-301

UNREALITY

UNREALITY

The Metaphysics of Fictional Objects

Charles Crittenden

Cornell University Press

Ithaca and London

Copyright © 1991 by Cornell University

All rights reserved. Except for brief quotations in a review, this book, or parts thereof, must not be reproduced in any form without permission in writing from the publisher. For information, address Cornell University Press, 124 Roberts Place, Ithaca, New York 14850.

First published 1991 by Cornell University Press.

International Standard Book Number 0-8014-2520-4 (cloth)
International Standard Book Number 0-8014-9754-X (paper)
Library of Congress Catalog Card Number 90-55739

Printed in the United States of America

Librarians: Library of Congress cataloging information appears on the last page of the book.

⊗ The paper in this book meets the minimum requirements of the American National Standard for Information Sciences—Permanence of Paper for Printed Library Materials, ANSI Z39.48-1984.

TO MY PARENTS

CONTENTS

PREFACE

The philosophical outlook of an era is reflected in the topics that attract the attention of its philosophers. I think it is fair to say that the problem of nonbeing, with which this book is occupied, has not been at the center of philosophical discussion since the early part of the century. Work has certainly been done on it, as the discussions to follow show; indeed there has been considerable interest in it lately. On the whole, however, the issue has been considered peripheral. There are several reasons for this situation, I believe.

The chief one is that professional philosophers in the West, like other mainstream professionals, have for the most part accepted the physical sciences as a model for knowledge and method. These sciences have been spectacularly successful in providing genuine understanding of important areas of reality. Furthermore, the technological products of this enterprise permeate Western society. If one takes scientific methodology and results as central, then one is likely to give little theoretical importance to such activities as telling stories, understanding myths, or reflecting on dreams; we somehow do these things, and we find them entertaining and relaxing, but the serious business of understanding reality must rely on hard-core scientific thought for its basic conceptions.

The second and more technical reason for the neglect of

nonbeing is that the conception of reference dominating recent thought has been one corresponding to, again, theory in the physical sciences For no doubt very good reasons, descriptive theories of reference have been replaced by explanations that assume a real connection between the thing referred to and the expression making the reference. Accompanying this relatively recent development has been the presumption that this connection ultimately must be explained in concrete, physical terms. This demand is encouraged by the tacit supposition that the object of reference must always be real and so presumably physical—no matter how things appear. The supposition itself is encouraged by the fact that the most successful sciences deal with the real—with what is present in space-time. So there is every reason to think that language apparently about the nonexistent will turn out, when correctly accounted for, to be about real things, explainable in terms of principles which, if not derived from the physical sciences, at least correspond to their practice.

Yet it happens, not unexpectedly, that language about the nonexistent does not lend itself to immediate explanation in terms of semantical conceptions reflecting these assumptions. Such items as fictional characters and mythical beings seem to be just plain nonexistent—simply not the sorts of thing the scientific framework is prepared to treat. Certainly one cannot explain the relation between a fictional character and a reference to it by assuming that somehow the former causes the latter, as is generally assumed for reference to real things: how can there be a causal relation between a nonexistent object and a reference to it? Current semantical explanations do not apply in any obvious way to fictional discourse. And so there is, perhaps, a tendency for philosophical attention to turn elsewhere, to problems more amenable to treatment in terms of the prevailing paradigm.

Yet it is just such neglected and "peripheral" issues, ones not readily explainable in terms of a current paradigm, which illuminate the thinking of a time and point up its weaknesses. This, I believe, is the case with the problem of nonbeing—at least with the attempt to explain fictional discourse in terms of contemporary doctrines in the philosophy of language. At any rate, fiction provides a wonderfully interesting test case. The concepts basic to the account presented in this book are different in important respects from those characteristic of current semantical theory, and they are connected with an overall outlook quite different from the one currently dominating the philosophical scene. If it is indeed the case that principles basic to the favored philosophy of language do not function well in resolving the various issues that concern nonbeing, then we might well think about the correctness of these principles and the paradigm that encourages them.

The problem of nonbeing attracted me very early on; I still have a piece of doggerel, set down in an idle undergraduate moment, about Something and Nothing. These two friends were out walking one day, discussing their problems. Nothing's difficulties were eventually traced to his not being there at all—certainly a serious matter. Whatever the merits of this piece as literature, it shows my sympathy for the plight of the nonexistent, now grown into a full-blown diagnosis, even if (from Nothing's standpoint) still offering no cure. A seminar on intentionality at the University of North Carolina at Chapel Hill by Everett W. Hall provided a more formal opportunity to become acquainted with the nonexistent. P. F. Strawson's lectures at Duke University, later to become *Individuals*, included a speech act theory of reference. These notions lay dormant until the time arrived for a dissertation, when eventually the topic of reference and fiction proved viable. Max Black provided tough and demanding yet patient and supportive direction, it is a source of deep regret that he will not be able to see the fully developed form of these ideas

Although I have been able to adopt some of my early work to the present study, my thinking has grown and deepened immeasurably through further reflection. One kind of stimulus has been the work of others. I mention in particular the lectures on fiction delivered by Saul Kripke at Harvard University in the fall of 1967. Kripke's analyses were astounding to me in their scope and depth, and it was only through struggling with his conceptions over a long period that I came to think that my basic approach is correct. Kripke is one thinker who has not avoided the problems posed by fiction for a causal theory of reference; it is certainly to be hoped that his work on fiction will eventually be published. Another stimulus is my interest in Eastern philosophy, particularly Buddhism, which takes an approach to fiction quite unlike that of Western thought. It is unfortunate that Eastern philosophy is not taken seriously in Western professional philosophical training; it has conceptions and emphases of great value which are almost entirely ignored in the West. This book illustrates my view that Western techniques and results and Eastern insights can each have a place in an overall outlook.

Certain very real individuals are due thanks for various kinds of assistance. Jerome Richfield was the best of all possible deans during most of my stay at California State University, Northridge, and I take this opportunity to thank him publicly for his support. Discussions with Laurie Calhoun, Keith Donnellan, Dan Hunter, Ian McFeteridge, Robert Martin, Terence Parsons, Bergeth Schroeder, and my Northridge students have been invaluable. I have benefited from the comments of readers for Cornell University Press, and from certain other readers unknown to me. The encouragement of John Ackerman of Cornell has meant a great deal. Finally, Daniel Sedey has been able not

only to arrange occasional partial alleviation of a heavy
teaching schedule but also to provide useful criticisms of
an earlier version of this work. For these and other kinds of
assistance far beyond the call of the duties of chairing a
large and sometimes divergent department, I want to express my deep gratitude.

Earlier versions of some of the material in Chapter 1 appeared in "Ontology and the Theory of Descriptions," *Philosophy and Phenomenological Research* 31 (1970):85–96.
Both "Fictional Existence," *American Philosophical Quarterly* 3 (1966):317–321, and "Thinking about Non-Being,"
Inquiry 16 (1973):290–312, contained brief statements of
some of the theses of Chapters 2, 3, and 4. The claims of
"Fictional Characters and Logical Completeness," *Poetics*
11 (1982):331–344, are much the same as those of the second section of Chapter 6, but the supporting arguments are
very different. "Everyday Reality as Fiction: A Madhyamika Interpretation," *Journal of Indian Philosophy* 9
(1981):323–333, elaborates some of the remarks of the second and third sections of Chapter 7.

CHARLES CRITTENDEN

Northridge, California

I

REFERENCE AND NONEXISTENCE
IN THE TWENTIETH CENTURY

In this book I consider the ancient problem of nonbeing, the problem whether there are nonexistent objects. Holding that there are seems to imply the contradiction that there exist things that do not exist. On the other hand, in common parlance we very often speak of things that do not exist. Sherlock Holmes does not exist, he is a fictional character. Pegasus is mythical and hence nonexistent. Phlogiston has turned out not to exist. Extinct species no longer exist, future items do not exist yet, there are all sorts of possible things that do not exist. Atheists certainly believe that God does not exist. So we employ the notion of nonexistence widely and quite comfortably. Furthermore, nonexistent things seem to have properties: Sherlock Holmes is a detective who plays the violin, he is not a banker; Pegasus is a winged horse, not a flying fish. The appearance is that ordinary discourse is committed to items that are somehow there and have properties, and yet are said not to exist. Does common language then assume contradictory entities? Surely there cannot *be* such things. But if not, what are we talking about in these cases? This is a tangle indeed; my purpose in this book is to sort through the strands wound together here and to use the resulting clarifications to deal with various philosophical issues.

As far as common thinking goes, fictional characters are among the nonexistent. Nevertheless, we are extremely familiar with literary fictions and probably feel we understand them about as well as we understand anything. This familiarity can be put to good philosophical use, for if our actual thinking about fictions can be brought out and made clear, considerable light should be thrown on the puzzle of nonbeing. I take it that this thinking is reflected in the language commonly employed concerning fiction. Writing stories, describing the contents of novels, stating opinions about characters, and comparing different works all incorporate just the distinctions constituting our conception of fiction. Indeed such language is definitive of this conception: to gain clarity about the distinctions and principles appearing in discourse concerning fiction *is* to understand everyday thought about fictions. This discourse, being generally accepted and practiced, constitutes a marvelously rich conceptual deposit awaiting philosophical excavation.

Surprisingly, this set of data has rarely been thoroughly studied. Fictional characters and mythical creatures have often been used as examples in philosophical discussions, but the general body of discourse in which these examples are naturally embedded has rarely been seriously examined. As a result, discussions of nonbeing have ignored conceptions and distinctions incorporated into actual practice in favor of a priori views about meaning or reference, or else quite cursory and inadequate analyses of everyday thought have been sketched—usually to suit the demands of theory and often with the consequence that ordinary thinking is dismissed as incorporating philosophically unacceptable commitments. The project I have undertaken starts with a different view of common language. By carefully bringing out the conceptions and distinctions found in ordinary discourse, I expose the logical categories and rules actually employed about nonexistence, and from this a solution to the problem of nonbeing emerges. Ordinary thought turns out, I believe, to contain a complex and subtle set of concepts constituting a quite adequate position on nonexistence; it is not at all the confused and philosophically flawed scheme its detractors have alleged. This chapter has two sections. The first is devoted to an account of this century's most important solutions to the problem of nonbeing, the strategies whereby these solutions were reached, and the goals intended to be served by following these strategies. Discussion here is primarily historical and metaphilosophical, intended to give a broad overview of representative positions. The reason for including more methodological material than is customary in a basically analytical account is that the important positions diverge not only in technical details but in general philosophical goals. A full grasp of the differences between them must therefore take these wider contrasts into account. Certainly I want my analysis to be understood not only in regard to its details but also in the light of the broader project I am undertaking; these metaphilosophical remarks provide this background.

In the second section of the chapter I consider the single most influential discussion of the nonexistence problem in this century, Russell's theory of descriptions. Since common language has commitments that it could not have if Russell's theory were true of it, it is important to show that Russell's theory does not give an accurate exposition of the ordinary speech situation. These two discussions— of the history and metaphilosophy of twentieth-century analytic thought, and of Russell's proposal—clear the ground for the positive account presented in the remainder of the book.

SOLUTIONS AND STRATEGIES

The first important figure in the debate over the nonexistent was Meinong. Meinong's teacher Brentano was interested in finding a clear dividing line between the mental and the physical This difference lay, Brentano thought, in the fact that mental phenomena are directed to or about objects—a point he took from the scholastics.[1] He did not accept the possibility of unreal objects, and to deal with the problem of nonexistence he formulated this principle: for every sentence apparently about a nonexistent object, "one can form an equivalent in which the subject and predicate are replaced by something referring to a real thing."[2] If all references in sentences ostensibly about nonexistent objects turn out to be about real things, then any reason to assume nonexistent objects has disappeared. This strategy became the basis for the first major deflationary approach to the problem of nonbeing. Meinong, on the other hand, held that the fact that we can think about both real and unreal things showed that "the totality of what exists, including what has existed and what will exist, is infinitely small in comparison with the totality of objects."[3] There is an entire subject matter that the empirical sciences, being largely committed to existence, ignore. The study of this grand totality of objects Meinong called Gegenstandtheorie, theory of objects. Meinong supposed that whatever can be thought about is an object, and he believed that something is an object if it satisfies some such principle as the following: x is an object if it corresponds to a definite or indefinite description (one having the form "the F" or "an F") appearing in a grammatically correct sentence having a truth value. Put more briefly, every grammatically acceptable definite or indefinite description designates an object.

1 See Franz Brentano, "The Distinction between Mental and Physical Phenomena," in Realism and the Background of Phenomenology, ed. Roderick M. Chisholm (Glencoe, Ill.: Free Press, 1960), p. 50.
2 Franz Brentano, Psychologie von empirischen Standpunkt, Vol. 2 (Leipzig, 1874), p. 163; quoted by Roderick M. Chisholm in "Franz Brentano," Encyclopedia of Philosophy, vol. 1, ed. Paul Edwards (New York: Macmillan, 1967), p. 367.
3 Quoted by Chisholm, Realism and the Background of Phenomenology, p. 6.

As Meinong employed it, this criterion admits as an object anything of any possible description or ontological category whatever. It admits, for example, the golden mountain (which satisfies the principle because it is true that it is both mountainous and golden) and, more peculiar, the round square (because the sentence "the round square is round" is true)—to mention Meinong's own famous examples and his reasoning supporting them.[4]

Meinong's conception of a discipline having as subject matter all objects of thought as such introduces an interesting perspective: to take for study, not just what exists, but whatever can be thought about regardless of existential status. Philosophers and scientists have traditionally been interested in what exists; metaphysics and the physical sciences take existing things as their subject matter. Meinong

---

4 Alexius Meinong, "Theory of Objects," in Chisholm, *Realism and the Background of Phenomenology*, p. 82. As far as I know, Meinong himself did not provide an explicit formulation of his criterion of objecthood. I attribute the above principle to him on the basis of the cases of nonexistent objects he accepted. This principle should be taken as only a sufficient condition of objecthood, since he admits objects not satisfying it, at least not in any natural way. I remark that as Meinong employs it, the principle leads to the admission of innumerable objects; one could avoid this consequence in various ways, one of them being to deny that such sentences as "The golden mountain is golden" and "The round square is round" have a truth value. Meinong appears to be relying at least partly on linguistic considerations to support his theories (e.g., truth values of assertions apparently about the nonexistent); in Chapter 2 I develop a criterion for objecthood also based on common language although, as developed, it is at odds with other commitments Meinong has made. For general discussions of Meinong see J. N. Findlay, *Meinong's Theory of Objects and Values*, 2d ed. (Oxford: Clarendon Press, 1963); the articles in *Jenseits von Sein und Nichtsein: Beitrage zur Meinong-Forschung*, ed. Rudolph Haller (Graz, Austria: Akademische Druck-u. Verlagsanstalt,1972); Reinhardt Grossman, *Meinong* (London: Routledge and Kegan Paul, 1974); David F. Lindenfeld, *The Transformation of Positivism: Alexius Meinong and European Thought, 1880–1920* (Berkeley: University of California Press, 1980); Karel Lambert, *Meinong and the Principle of Independence: Its Place in Meinong's Theory of Objects and Its Significance in Contemporary Philosophical Logic* (Cambridge: Cambridge University Press, 1983); and the writings of Roderick M. Chisholm already cited.

has noticed that common thinking ranges far beyond this: in actual practice, much of our attention concerns what does not exist or what is not known or even assumed to exist, or it concerns items where the existence/nonexistence distinction applies only obscurely. With his theory of objects Meinong does not attempt particularly to explain how it happens that there are nonexisting objects or to justify accepting them; he aims rather at classifying nonexistent items and indicating differences among them. The theory is therefore vulnerable to the charge that there are no nonexistent entities; there are only the things that the sciences or metaphysics address, and so the theory collapses into these more traditional disciplines. Various consequences of Meinong's assumptions seem to support this judgment. There is the implication that there are, in his liberal sense of "there are," realm upon unfathomable realm of objects, extending far beyond anything imagined by the most generous philosopher. Meinong must admit as objects not only all the numbers and various kinds of abstractions that could ever be enumerated but also all the fictional or mythical beings that could ever appear in stories. Plato's realm of Forms, to mention one metaphysically generous theory, would constitute just one relatively small kingdom in the vast empire defined by Meinong's theory of objects. Even more remarkable is the category of incomplete objects, illustrated by the golden mountain that has only the properties mentioned in its denoting phrase (being golden and being a mountain). Perhaps oddest of all are contradictory objects such as the round square. Given the numbers and peculiarities of the entities Meinong accepts, Russell's reaction is understandable: "In such theories, it seems to me, there is a failure of that feeling for reality which ought to be preserved even in the most abstract studies."[5] These consequences of Meinong's liberal

---

5 Bertrand Russell, *Introduction to Mathematical Philosophy* (London: George Allen and Unwin, 1956), p. 169.

admissions policy may suggest that it is a mistake to grant that there is anything nonexistent at all. Yet this reaction would be extreme, for it leaves the linguistic grounds for Meinong's claims unaccounted for. There is a position, I argue, that admits nonexistent objects without allowing them in unrestricted numbers and also avoids other objec tionable features of Meinong's views. But whatever the merits of his own solution, it is clear that Meinong has identified a genuine philosophical problem.

It may be helpful at this point to comment on Meinong's original conception of his discipline. As noted, the theory of objects takes seriously the fact that in actual discourse we really do talk about, in a familiar sense of "talk about," various species of nonexistent object. Surely Meinong is right in supposing that this fact is something of which an account is appropriate. Such an account could classify the kinds of conceptual status these objects are taken as having and perhaps indicate various logical relationships among them. There is no reason to fault the theory of objects for having these goals. On the other hand—to outline consid-erations to be elaborated later—the types of object Mei-nong has admitted as an appropriate subject matter extend far beyond those that actual linguistic practice accepts. We can imagine contexts in which one might refer to a golden mountain (headline in newspaper: "Geologists Find Golden Mountain in Colorado") or perhaps even a round square (opening line of a "logic fiction" short story: "One day Johnny found a round-square hoop which he rolled and bumped home to show his mother"). But it would require such practical contexts to make everyday references to such odd items acceptable. If one were simply to remark casually, without providing any setting, "the golden moun-tain is golden, you know" or "the round square is round," this would be met with puzzlement and a request for fur-ther explanation ("*Is* there a golden mountain?—what are you talking about?"; "What in the world do you mean, 'round square'?"). In practice, reference is always within a

context, and the objects denoted there must have been introduced into that context in some way or other—fictional
characters, for instance, are always introduced into a story
by the author's writing about them. Such considerations
as these must be included in any account of reference and
objects spoken about. Meinong has completely neglected
contextual considerations, and this neglect has resulted in
consequences that have been thought to discredit his enterprise altogether. His test for what counts as an object, for
example, is purely grammatical or syntactical (or so
he is naturally construed): any expression having a certain form and appearing in a grammatically acceptable sentence designates an object. "Golden mountain" and "round
square" meet the test; thus there are objects corresponding
to them and the philosophical hackles begin to rise. It is
also this test that allows the admission of any number of
objects; clearly as many denoting expressions as you like
are formulable, and so indefinitely many objects are admitted.[6] A natural suggestion here is that constraints on what
counts as an object should not be purely grammatical but
should include relevant features of the speech situation. If
such a criterion were employed, neither such logically peculiar objects as golden mountains and round squares nor
an indefinitely large number of objects would be admitted.
Or, if they were admitted, the circumstances under which
this occurred would make them quite philosophically re-

6 One wonders what expressions would *fail* the test. Presumably
strings of linguistic symbols simply concatenated would fail, but how
about expressions that are syntactically in order but include category violations, for instance, "the green prime number" in "The green prime number is green," or overt nonsense items "about" which something is said
("momeraths," said by Lewis Carroll to "outgrabe")? If round squares are
acceptable, then it appears that green prime numbers and momeraths
must be allowed too. Such cases make it imperative for those sympathetic
to Meinong to provide some principled way of excluding or at least explaining them while admitting the more standard instances. The position
I present provides such a way.

spectable. Developing such a view is the burden of later chapters.

Russell took an entirely different route. At first agreeing with Meinong that there are nonexistent entities, he later changed his mind and proposed his deflationary theory of descriptions. Later I discuss this theory at length; for now it is sufficient to say that it incorporates the same principle that Brentano adopted, namely, that for every sentence containing an expression apparently referring to a nonexistent entity a paraphrase can be found not containing such a reference. Thus there is no need to assume the realms of the nonexistent postulated by Meinong. But Russell did not merely offer this procedure for avoiding nonexistent objects; he also gave internal criticisms of Meinong's position. It is clear that Russell was not led to eliminate nonexistent objects chiefly on grounds of simplicity or other broad theoretical criteria, which would be a more contemporary rationale; rather, his justification lay in what he felt were immediate difficulties in Meinong's account. First, as he remarked in the 1905 presentation of his theory of descriptions, to suppose that there are objects such as the present King of France and the round square, which do not even subsist, "is a difficult view."[7] The particular view of Meinong's which Russell is criticizing is, not that there *are* objects such as the round square and the present King of France, but that these do not even subsist. Subsistence is a form of Being—the most general existential category—belonging to "ideal" objects such as numbers and such items as similarity and difference; Meinong held the principle of Aussersein, the independence of Being (*sein*) in any form from having properties (*so-sein*);[8] Russell's point seems to

---

7 Bertrand Russell, "On Denoting," in *Logic and Knowledge*, ed. Robert C. Marsh (London: George Allen and Unwin, 1956), p. 45.

8 See Meinong, "Theory of Objects." For further elaboration, see Roderick M. Chisholm, "Beyond Being and Nonbeing," in *Jenseits von Sein und Nichtsein*, pp. 25–36.

be that denying items any foothold in reality whatever makes it unreasonable to consider them objects at all. This claim is a metaphysical one, evidently based on the principle that if something is an object then it must have at least some degree or kind of reality even if not having concrete existence.

Russell's chief objection of 1905, however, was that the objects admitted by Meinong's principle of objecthood "are apt to infringe the law of contradiction": the existent present King of France (Russell's example) exists and also does not exist, the round square is round and also not round. "But this is intolerable," Russell remarked; for him the laws of logic were inviolable.[9] A third objection, not presented until 1919, was that Meinong's theory violates a "robust sense of reality" because what exists in regard to myth or fiction is merely the thought processes of the person thinking about such things. There is only one world, the real one, and it does not include Hamlet but only Shakespeare's mental states as he wrote the play or ours as we view it. Logic ought not to admit unrealities such as unicorns any more than the empirical sciences do, for "logic is concerned with the real world just as truly as zoology" or any other empirical field.[10] One might wonder how this claim squares with Russell's earlier analyses, for now it appears that strictly accurate paraphrases must denote the mental contents of those who entertain thoughts about nonexistent objects rather than the public, historical entities referred to in the instances of paraphrases Russell gave earlier. Finally, a number of years later Russell offered a fourth objection related to the preceding three: "Common

9 Russell, "On Denoting," p. 45. Meinong's response was that the law of contradiction holds only for what is real and not for objects (such as the round square) that do not belong to any category of existence whatever. This reply gains support from considerations to be offered later, especially in the last section of Chapter 6.

10 Russell, *Introduction to Mathematical Philosophy*, pp. 169–170.

speech is full of vagueness and inaccuracy," and "any attempt to be precise and accurate requires modification of common speech both as regards vocabulary and syntax."[11] Such an attempt requires modification of syntax because the philosopher or logician may well be "misled by grammar" in that he is likely to "have regarded grammatical form as a surer guide in analysis than in fact it is." What is required with regard to the problem of nonexistence is "to find a more accurate and analysed thought to replace the somewhat confused thought which most people at most times have in their heads"—to provide suitable sentences not denoting nonexistent objects.[12] As becomes apparent in the following chapters, I disagree with Russell on all four of these counts.

It is worth taking a moment here to reflect on the different attitudes adopted by Russell and Meinong on ordinary expressions referring to the nonexistent, for these expressions are the main focus in the chapters to come. Meinong's position was that, since such expressions do apparently denote nonexistent objects, there must be such things. Russell on the other hand believed that admitting the nonexistent led to too many theoretical problems; the more reasonable position was that despite linguistic appearances there are no such objects. It followed that expressions seemingly denoting them are misleading and should be replaced in a philosophically correct language. The position I develop agrees with Meinong's that in general ordinary expressions referring to the nonexistent are perfectly sound as they are commonly used and not metaphysically flawed, and thus that there are nonexistent objects; it sides with Russell's in granting that there are not the vast realms of nonexistent objects Meinong accepted and that one must

11 Bertrand Russell, "Mr. Strawson on Referring," in *My Philosophical Development* (New York: Simon and Schuster, 1959), pp. 241–242.
12 Ibid., p. 243.

look beyond the syntactical forms of the expressions themselves to discover when there is genuine reference to the
nonexistent. Unlike Russell, however, I believe that what
we must look beyond syntax to is not the possibility of a
paraphrase revealing a supposed logical form but the speech
context in which such reference is made. Working this position out leads to a view that has something in common
with each of these opposing analyses.

For a deeper understanding of Russell's solution to the
problem of nonbeing we must look at the larger goals of the
tradition initiated with the theory of descriptions and its
allied doctrines. Basic planks in this tradition are that logic
is concerned with the real world in very much the same
way as are the empirical sciences, and that one of the tasks
of the philosopher is to find forms of language superior to
those of everyday speech, where these improvements are to
incorporate the structures of formal logic. Russell's own
way of implementing these principles lay in the program of
logical atomism, which conceived the world as made up of
atomic facts whose constituents are the ultimate elements
of being and which are denoted by the meaningful units of
language. Analysis utilizing quantificational logic has the
central methodological role here, and by illustrating the
analysis of a proposition into its basic terms and thereby
solving a philosophical problem, the theory of descriptions
could serve as a showpiece.[13] Ultimately, logical atomism
began to lose its appeal. For one thing, the very idea of an
"atomic fact" came to seem dubious since there was no
clearly nonarbitrary way of identifying such things or the
elements that constitute them; for another, "logical form"
began to seem more and more elusive. But these and other
problems with logical atomism did not diminish the attrac-
tion of the theory of descriptions as a method for dealing
with issues of nonbeing; this solution retained its popu-

13 For discussion of various aspects of logical atomism, see J. O.
Urmson, *Philosophical Analysis: Its Development between the Two
World Wars* (Oxford: Oxford University Press, 1956).

larity despite the demise of the program it initially served to illustrate. Those attracted to formal analysis eventually abandoned logical atomism and conceived the philosophical enterprise in other terms; here Quine can serve as the representative of the emerging position.

Quine extends the test implicit in Russell's procedure to a general criterion for ontological commitment: "A theory is committed to those and only those entities to which the bound variables of the theory must be capable of referring in order that the affirmations made in the theory be true."[14] But this is only a formal criterion; there is still the question of which type of theory the criterion is to be applied to. Here Quine sees science as authoritative: "Our ontology is determined once we have fixed upon the over-all conceptual scheme which is to accommodate science in the broadest sense."[15] The contents of this scheme are to be decided by invoking what Quine regards as the standard criteria for evaluating theories: simplicity, familiarity of principle, scope, fecundity, and success in predicting.[16] He speculates that when these criteria are applied it will turn out that a physicalistic scheme (supplemented with classes) ranks higher than its competitors—that it will be physicalistic entities over which the bound variables in formalized versions of successful scientific theory range.[17]

14 Willard Van Orman Quine, "On What There Is," in *From a Logical Point of View* (Cambridge, Mass.: Harvard University Press, 1953), pp. 13–14.

15 Ibid., pp. 16–17.

16 W. V. Quine, *Ways of Paradox and Other Essays* (New York: Random House, 1966), p. 234. Other such lists are found elsewhere in Quine's writings.

17 The chief alternative, Quine thinks, is a phenomenalistic framework; nevertheless, even considering its advantages, "we should still find, no doubt, that a physicalistic conceptual scheme, purporting to talk about external objects, offers great advantages in simplifying our over-all reports"; "On What There Is," p. 17. This is a relatively early statement, but Quine's basic stand has never changed; see, e.g., "Things and Their Place in Theories," in *Theories and Things* (Cambridge, Mass.: Harvard University Press, 1981).

Quine is envisioning a single, unified theoretical structure for which in its idealized form quantificational logic supplies both syntax and referential apparatus and consequently provides the test of ontological commitment. Of course there will not be quantification over nonexistent entities; if Quine's speculations arc right, only physical things will be denoted. We might see this view as the completion of Russell's program of constructing a single, general explanation grounded in science and replacing ordinary syntactical and semantical forms regarded as misleading.

Or perhaps we might see this view as *one* way of completing Russell's project; in fact, the various strands in his outlook can be woven together in rather different ways. I mention Quine particularly because he is heavily indebted to Russell and because his work has been so influential; his writings have more or less defined orthodoxy for the Russellian tradition for the past few decades. Recently, however, others within this tradition have taken a different stand on the issue of nonbeing. Terence Parsons has made an important contribution here; I discuss his proposals at length in Chapter 5. Here his general stance is of interest. He writes that, although he first accepted the theory of descriptions, he began to become attracted to Meinong's position. As a result, he developed an alternative way of dealing with the problem of nonexistent objects, one employing Quinean criteria of theory construction but admitting nonexistent objects. This approach allows him to remain within the orthodox tradition while holding a theory "inconsistent with the orthodox view."[18] Because of his adherence to the general aims and methodology of the Russell–Quine enterprise, he can count himself an adherent of this

18 Terence Parsons, *Nonexistent Objects* (New Haven, Conn.: Yale University Press, 1980), p. 9. The interesting description of his gradual conversion to a Meinongian viewpoint is given in the preface, pp. xi–xiii. See pp. 5–9 for his perceptive remarks on the status of Meinongian theories in contemporary academic Anglo-American philosophy.

tradition even though rejecting the standard paraphrase solution to the problem of nonbeing.

The possibility within the mainstream Russellian position of the kind of view Parsons proposes signals a shift in
basic criteria for theory acceptability. Russell relied on
what he thought of as immediately evident and clear-cut
objections to the proposal that there are nonexistent objects; similarly, he supposed that his paraphrase technique
could be understood by any reasonable and philosophically
sophisticated individual to provide propositions equivalent
in meaning to those ostensibly about nonexistent objects.
Russell adopted traditional standards for evaluating theories: they are to be judged by their ability to give an account of the facts central to an issue and to withstand objections. These are matters that can be judged relatively
quickly on the basis of clearheaded reflection on a fairly
limited and more or less immediately available set of considerations. No appeal to broad theoretical considerations
or to long periods of testing is required. Parsons, however,
invokes a different set of methodological considerations.
Despite certain objectionable features, "the orthodox view
is a fine view; it has been extremely useful."[19] But an unor-
thodox view actually admitting nonexistent objects has
much going for it too, "enough reason, *prima facie* to believe in them, to make it worthwhile to try to develop a
theory about them, *with a reasonable hope that it will*

19 Ibid., p. 8. Notice that Russell, despite having accepted Meinong's
views at an earlier stage, would not have made such a remark about them.
For Russell, a theory either gives a correct analysis or it does not—there is
no question of different proposals suggesting diverging research programs
to be evaluated only after lengthy study. Whether a theory does give the
right analysis can be decided on the basis of reflection on a relatively
small number of logical issues by sophisticated individuals. Applying the
relevant criteria, Russell has found that Meinong's views are clearly
wrong and this ends the matter—at least it does unless flaws in Russell's
reasoning can be found. For Russell, philosophy is still a conceptual enterprise and has methods distinct from those of the physical sciences.

turn out to be true." This outcome cannot be determined by simple reflection: "Whether it *is* true or not will ultimately be decided in terms of global considerations how well it accords with the data and with other theories, and how widespread and interesting its applications are. Only years of use and critical examination can answer such questions."[21] We have moved a long way from the claim that philosophical disputes can be resolved by considering a few crucial arguments. Now we must examine competing global hypotheses at great length and only decide between them after years of use and critical examination. Perhaps the difference here reflects the replacement of mathematics or formal logic as the model for philosophical procedure by the physical sciences. Still, this is a change within the overall program of attempting to construct a general outlook based on technical considerations and so to improve on ordinary thinking; the goals of the program Russell inaugurated remain in force for Parsons and so differ from those guiding the present study. Something must be said about this latter now.

Strawson makes a useful distinction between "descriptive" and "revisionary" metaphysics, the former being "content to describe the actual structure of our thought about the world" whereas the latter is "concerned to produce a better structure."[22] In terms of this distinction, Meinong is a descriptivist: he intended to give an account of the kinds of object that he believed were ignored by science but acknowledged by common thought. He is, however, at the same time a realist about the nonexistent, since for him the items with which the theory of objects was concerned have their status quite apart from whether "our thought about the world" actually recognizes them;

20 Ibid., pp. 37–38.
21 Ibid., p. 38.
22 P. F. Strawson, *Individuals: An Essay in Descriptive Metaphysics* (London: Methuen, 1959), p. 9.

certainly he would have rejected any suggestion that what the theory of objects studies are merely a function of our thought. He also held that there is a correspondence between everyday language and his nonexistent objects and certainly did not believe that such language is for this reason in need of replacement. Russell's theory of descriptions, on the other hand, is one of the paradigms of the revisionist program and reflects its originator's view that everyday thought about the nonexistent is somewhat confused. Parsons, though accepting Russell's technical methods and aim of producing a better outlook, takes a step in the direction of the Meinongian and descriptivist camp, since he is willing to admit that there is nothing wrong with ordinary expressions seeming to denote nonexistent objects. Or perhaps it is more accurate to report him as holding that, at present, before working out all the ramifications of the competing Meinongian and eliminationist proposals, we do not know whether there is anything wrong with these expressions and so are justified in taking their implications at face value. The theory of descriptions represents one of the major alternatives, but there is the possibility that Russell judged too quickly that Meinong was wrong. Parsons is in the interesting position of rejecting, or at least questioning, a paradigm—in the Kuhnian sense—of a tradition in which Parsons locates himself.[23] In

23 On Kuhnian theory this would appear impossible since paradigms define their traditions—but I leave the resolution of this matter to others. I should mention that Parsons is not the only contemporary philosopher to argue for Meinongian conclusions on the basis of broad theoretical considerations. Hector-Neri Castañeda offers a comparable theory, one he embeds in his more general theory of individuals. See his "Fiction and Reality: Their Fundamental Connections," *Poetics* 8 (1979):31–62, and also his *On Philosophical Method* (*Nous* Publications no. 1, 1980) for a discussion of his methodology. A full discussion of Castañeda's views on fiction would require consideration of his broader theory of individuals, too much to undertake here. Robert Howell, "Fictional Objects: How They Are and How They Aren't," *Poetics* 8 (1979):175, offers criticism of Castañeda's proposals on fiction.

any case, Parsons's attitude toward ordinary language is quite different from Russell's and not necessarily revisionist—ordinary language *could* turn out to embody the best account of nonexistent objects. In Chapter 5 I discuss the success of Parsons's attempt to include such objects within the orbit of the Russellian program.

My position in this study is descriptivist (with a qualification to appear shortly), and this is the place to indicate what is to be achieved from this stance. In the first place, from the perspective of the problem of nonbeing, it can offer a solution. Drawing out conceptions implicit in everyday talk about the nonexistent brings to light criteria, distinctions, and principles actually in force, and when these are perspicuously arranged they provide a way of resolving the difficulties mentioned at the outset of this chapter. The problem is solved simply by making clear the concepts employed in everyday use. This procedure serves the further purpose of a defense of ordinary thought, for as indicated a primary motivation for revisionism has been the elimination of supposed philosophical difficulties inherent in ordinary talk about the nonexistent. This motivation is misguided if included in common thought are materials that can be organized into a solution to these difficulties. At this point I can only claim that everyday thought contains the materials for a constructive solution; the support for this claim must lie in the details of the arguments to follow.

Yet some might feel that, even if common thinking can provide a solution, there is still a question as to its ultimate value: is this answer any better than others? Is there any particular merit to a solution reflecting common thought? There are two parts to my response on this. First, I am sympathetic with the Wittgensteinian view that philosophical puzzlement arises through a misunderstanding of ordinary concepts; thus problems about nonexistence occur because of a failure to understand notions commonly used with regard to the nonexistent. From this standpoint the problem is dealt with through making these concepts clear and showing in detail just how they apply in areas generating confusion. Second, there is another perspective on this problem not incompatible with the first: that the philosopher has a natural and healthy desire to have a view of things in general, including an overview of our conceptual framework. This is satisfied, for the problem of nonbeing, by discovering broad conceptual regularities and noting their application to issues of nonexistence. Perhaps Wittgenstein himself did not feel any need to arrive at any such general outlook; for him philosophical therapy is enough. Nevertheless, it seems to me that particular points of usage advanced to remove conceptual confusion may, at least for some issues, be subject to arrangement into a general overview of the relevant conceptual terrain. Such an overview may make the therapy more effective by showing how a particular point of clarification has its place in a broader perspective and thus provide a further reason for resisting a tempting but mistaken conception. In any case, the project of descriptive metaphysics is not theorizing on the model of science, something Wittgenstein was particularly concerned to reject, but conceptual analysis on a broad scale; at least to this extent Wittgenstein's strictures against theorizing are observed.[24] Given this conception, philosophical theory is possible, as indeed most philosophers in the Western tradition have believed, and in this regard this study belongs to this tradition. So I view the various conceptual considerations to be brought forth as useful on the one hand in dispelling philosophical puzzlement, but on the other as reflecting aspects of our general

24 Some of these matters are discussed in my "Wittgenstein on Philosophical Therapy and Understanding," *International Philosophical Quarterly* 10 (1970):20–43. See also G. P. Baker and P. M. S. Hacker, *Wittgenstein: Understanding and Meaning* (Chicago: University of Chicago Press, 1980), pp. 488–491.

framework which can be arranged so as to constitute a constructive solution to the problem of nonbeing. Indeed this
solution avoids objections attendant on its competitors, as
I argue throughout; in this sense I offer a good and arguably
the best such solution.

There is another consideration to be mentioned here—
but one too large to pursue. On my view, common language has conceptual priority over any other proposed
scheme, including that of the natural sciences. This view
of the status of everyday thought goes beyond Strawson's
descriptive conception of it and claims that our scheme or
ones counterpart to it are the only possible ones.[25] If they
are, philosophical thinking must be broadly in terms of
common thought as opposed to fitting with revisionary criteria, a condition my solution meets. But issues here are
too ramified for me to make more than this remark about
them.

There is one further matter calling for comment. Much
of the recent philosophical attention to fiction has been in
the interest of constructing a formal semantics for fictional
discourse. For several reasons the present study does not
attempt to contribute to this enterprise. First, this would
require a long excursion into a set of technical issues quite
unlike those that are the central focus here. Even if a formal semantics of fictional discourse is possible—in itself a
controversial matter on which I take no stand—it will require clarification of the regularities and distinctions embedded in common practice. So discussions of the type offered here can be regarded as a necessary preliminary to a
formal treatment. Second, it should be clear from the remarks in the paragraphs just above that this study is in the
tradition of ordinary language philosophy, with its emphasis on particular points of usage, the importance of con-

25 This claim is argued in my "Transcendental Arguments Revived,"
Philosophical Investigations 8 (1985):229–251.

text, sensitivity to differences in types of discourse, interest in speaker's intentions, and the like. Setting out the regularities of common discourse in these terms is illuminating in itself, regardless of its contribution to a formalization. Indeed, historically the ordinary language approach has been suspicious of formal treatments, since these tend to ignore distinctions important to common usage; these suspicions are perhaps less warranted nowadays in view of the advent of free logic, relevance logic, and other comparable developments. Still, the results of my analysis are not expressed in the terms of truth functional semantics and are not straightforwardly translatable into them. Whether they can be so expressed is itself a large topic, somewhat aside from the project I am undertaking. Unlike some in the ordinary language tradition, I am not hostile to formal treatments and indeed have made suggestions toward their improvement.[26] In any case these are, to repeat, two different enterprises, and I am attempting only the former while leaving open the questions of whether the latter can be achieved and if so how.[27]

26 In "Ontology and the Theory of Descriptions," *Philosophy and Phenomenological Research* 31 (1970):85–96, I have commented on certain technical matters pertaining to formal logic: the proper reading of the existential quantifier and the interpretation of a bound variable in the light of my analysis of fictional objects.

27 Some might characterize the discussions I undertake in this study as pragmatics, as opposed to the semantics that a systematization in truth functional terms provides. They would feel that a such a semantics can be done independently of pragmatic considerations, which concern only details of practice and not matters of actual reference. This conception rejects the view expressed in the remarks above, that a study of usage is a prerequisite to developing a formal logic of fiction. Resolving this issue requires discussing deep questions concerning reference and the relation of language and reality, some of which are touched on in Chapter 3. Let me merely remark that reference is, in my view, a function of the use of terms governed by rules of actual practice and cannot be abstracted from them as the objection here assumes. In terms of the objection, semantics presupposes pragmatics and is not independent of it.

ELIMINATION BY PARAPHRASE:
THE THEORY OF DESCRIPTIONS

Russell's theory of descriptions incorporates the principle formulated by Brentano but with application particularly to names or definite descriptions: assertions containing such terms apparently denoting nonexisting entities can be paraphrased into statements that do not contain these expressions but instead assert the existence of these objects. Russell's famous example is

(1) The present [i.e., 1905] King of France is bald

which becomes, on applying the theory of descriptions,

(2) There is one and only one present King of France and he is bald

Proposition (2) is held to be equivalent in meaning to (1), which is thus exposed as the assertion of the existence of something that does not exist. So (1) is false and not nonsense, as "one would suppose."[28] This example represents the general case: there are no true assertions about nonexistent objects as Meinong held, there are only false ones implying that such objects exist. With this result Russell was "able to hold that there are no unreal individuals" and the problem of nonbeing was solved.[29]

Russell evidently meant his theory to apply to standard fictional and mythical characters;[30] this is a condition that any theory attempting to deal with the problem of nonbeing must meet. It is noteworthy that Russell's own exam-

28 Russell, "On Denoting," p. 46. The exact statement of paraphrase (2) is couched in the technical devices of mathematical logic; these are unimportant for present purposes and are omitted to simplify discussion.
29 Ibid., pp. 54–55.
30 Ibid., p. 54.

ple is not taken from literature at all—we are not to suppose that there is some recognizable fictional character that (1) concerns. In fact, the theory can hardly be taken as a plausible analysis of a statement about a genuine fictional being. Consider

(3) The chief cyclops lives in a cave

meant to be about the one-eyed monster encountered by Odysseus in the *Odyssey*. For Russell this statement would be equivalent to

(4) There exists one and only one chief cyclops and it lives in a cave

Russell would claim that (4) is false—there never had been a historical cyclops—and since (4) is simply a paraphrase of (3), the latter too must be false. But this result conflicts with our ordinary beliefs, for we take it as true that the chief cyclops in the *Odyssey* lives in a cave. For example, anyone who marked (3) false on an examination in classical literature would be counted wrong. Thus (3) and (4) have different truth values and so cannot have the same meaning. Because they have different truth values, (4) cannot be held to express the content of (3) and Russell is not in a position to claim that his paraphrase technique gives the actual content of statements apparently denoting nonexistent objects. But if he is not, then he has not shown that such expressions do not denote nonexistent objects—he has not given a solution to the problem of nonbeing.

The difficulty is that Russell's procedure applied to cases of recognized fiction or myth conflicts with accepted truths, and a defender of his theory might now try to show that this conflict is merely apparent and not real. One suggestion along these lines is that (3) has what in other contexts Russell calls "secondary" occurrence, that it falls under the scope of an operator, as we would say nowadays. The obvious candidate for the operator is "in the Odyssey," which gives

(3a) In the *Odyssey* the chief cyclops lives in a cave

Statement (3a) is unobjectionable as a reading of (3)—in fact, in Chapter 4 I argue that sentences of the type to which (3) belongs always assume such an operator. Now we are in a position to raise the crucial question: can the theory of descriptions be applied to (3a) with the result that this statement is true, as is commonly assumed? There are two interpretations of (3a) to be considered here, depending on whether the operator is to be given narrow or wide scope:

(3a1) There exists one and only one chief cyclops and in the *Odyssey* it lives in a cave
(3a2) In the *Odyssey* there is one and only chief cyclops and it lives in a cave

Statement (3a1) is not a plausible rendition—it asserts the historical existence of the cyclops, something not to be attributed to the *Odyssey* as a work of literature—so we are left with (3a2). Now we must question how this statement should be understood. Presumably the included clause, "there is one and only one chief cyclops and it lives in a cave," must turn out to be false; otherwise this clause is being read as truly asserting that there is a cyclops, and nonexistent entities have not been ruled out. Russell's basic move for eliminating such things—of turning apparent designations of them into false assertions of their existence—must surely be allowed to be played here. But if this clause if false, then presumably the *Odyssey* must be understood as claiming that there really was a cyclops who lived in a cave, of claiming this false proposition. This result is, however, perfectly acceptable, Russell's advocate might continue, since (3a2) as a whole is true: it is true that according to the *Odyssey* there exists a cyclops; the *Odyssey* does include this falsehood. And now we have what a vindication of the theory of descriptions requires, Russell's defender concludes, since (3), its expansion (3a), and the proper theoretical reading (3a2), are all true. Thus there is no conflict between applications of the theory of descriptions to assertions about fictions and accepted truth values.

This defense of Russell's theory will not do, for it requires an implausible interpretation of (3a2). On the interpretation implicit in the above argument, the *Odyssey* is read as claiming that the false proposition that there exists a cyclops is true. But this reading requires understanding this poem as a historical account, as about real things and events. This interpretation takes the *Odyssey* as making false claims about history, but as about history nevertheless. Yet no even moderately sophisticated person would understand this work as history; it is epic poetry. The writing in the relevant passages is plainly the product of the imagination and not meant to be understood as historical or even as necessarily having a historical basis. To take the relevant parts of the *Odyssey* as a report of a historical voyage, and to assume that they imply that there was some historical date and place at which this voyage occurred, would be to misunderstand the genre.[31] On such a reading these passages would have to be considered very bad reporting or journalism. One actually employing this way of re-

---

31 Even someone like Schliemann, who used Homer's poems in his astounding discovery of the historical Troy, would suppose that only some of the events in the epics had a historical basis. He would certainly not look for the cyclops's cave or its bones, for the features ascribed to this monster make it reasonably regarded as purely imaginary. That a work has passages some of which can be understood as based on actual fact does not require that every passage in the work must be taken as historical. There is still a place for judgment about how particular parts of a text are to be interpreted. Schliemann's great and successful innovation was to see *some* of Homer's writing as having a factual basis.

garding the *Odyssey* would hardly be able to adopt the mode of thinking appropriate to epic poems· of thinking of the writing as about a set of figures (Odysseus, his wife, members of his crew, the sirens) interacting in certain ways and having certain adventures. This familiar kind of consciousness, with its absorption in the story and characteristic reactions such as fear at what the cyclops might do to Odysseus and admiration and wonder at Odysseus' clever escape, would be impossible to achieve if the *Odyssey* were read as (even bad) history. So this defense of Russell's theory is committed to a misclassification of works of fiction as history and thus conflicts with ordinary belief. This is not a conflict in truth values but is clear and definite nevertheless. One can conclude that Russell's theory of descriptions has not been successfully defended against the accusation of not representing common thought. There may be other proposals for reconciling the theory with ordinarily accepted truths, but I think that the suggestion considered here is the most attractive one. I do not discuss others but pass to one further view incorporating the basic principle of paraphrase. This view turns out to be inadequate too.

A theory that crops up in conversation from time to time and has been recommended (though as far as I know not carefully elaborated) in the literature is that assertions seeming to be about fictional characters are really about authors and the sentences they write and not about characters and events in their fiction.[32] The paraphrase associated

<hr/>

32 Gilbert Ryle recommends such a theory in "Imaginary Objects," *Proceedings of the Aristotelian Society*, Supplementary Volume 12 (1933):18–43, and in "Systematically Misleading Expressions," reprinted in *Logic and Language (First and Second Series)*, ed. Antony Flew (Garden City, N.Y.: Anchor Books, 1965), pp. 13–40. He does not, however, formulate this proposal in a concrete way. Ryle also remarks that an author is only pretending to designate people with the "pseudo-designations" his sentences include. The proposal to attribute only pretended and not real reference to authors, but without basing this proposal on considerations of paraphrase, is one I examine at length in the next chapter.

with this proposal mentions the sentence in question; thus full expression of (3) is

(3b) Someone wrote a story containing "the chief cyclops lives in a cave" (or containing sentences implying this)

The point behind this suggestion is to deny reference to the definite description, for this is now said merely to be mentioned and not used since it appears in a sentence itself only mentioned. There is thus never reference to nonexistent objects; there is only the mention of referring expressions said to appear in books written by specific authors. This theory has the advantage of allowing there to be true statements concerning fictional items, as (3b), so one of the chief objections to the theory of descriptions and related views does not hold here.

It is fairly obvious that this suggestion does not work. Its central idea is that names in fiction are not used but only mentioned. On the face of it this looks most implausible, for names and the like in fiction certainly give the impression of having the same employment as they do in other contexts. Sentences making up works of fiction include exactly the same semantical devices (names, pronouns, demonstratives, cross-reference) as sentences outside fiction. If this impression is supported by an account of reference, then this proposal must be judged wrong; in Chapter 2 I offer just such an account of reference. Second, the theory is committed, for every occurrence of an expression apparently referring to a fiction, to the existence of a synonymous sentence merely mentioning the expression. This might seem easy enough for cases such as (3), where (3b) can serve—although there are problems even here, I believe—but what about instances like "the chief cyclops is the most interesting monster in Greek literature"? It is not even clear what candidates for a suitable paraphrase might be. It seems unlikely that any could be found, since on the face of it what interest is being expressed here is not in the

phrase "the chief cyclops" but in the chief cyclops. Any suggested paraphrase will at the very least be complex and unintuitive, and one seems entitled to doubt whether any satisfactory candidate can be found.
Perhaps a supporter of the no-reference view would appeal to certain criteria for reference widely accepted in contemporary philosophy. This suggestion would return us to

(3a) In the *Odyssey* the chief cyclops lives in a cave

The argument would be that "in the *Odyssey*" introduces a nonextensional context, and it is widely held that in such contexts names and denoting phrases do not have their usual reference. Since Frege, many philosophers have held that an expression has reference only if (a) coextensional terms can be substituted with preservation of truth value, and (b) existential generalization can be applied to the sentence including the expression. Expressions in nonextensional contexts fail these two tests, and since referring expressions concerning fictional items always occur in such contexts [illustrated by (3a)] they do not refer. Again we have the conclusion that there is no reference in works of fiction.

There are various replies to this set of contentions. For one, there is a question of the status of these two tests for reference; they presuppose doctrines that are themselves controversial, at least to my mind. In Chapter 2 I offer an account of reference appearing to have little relation to these two tests. It is, however, unnecessary to press this matter, since even given these tests one cannot conclude that there is always a failure of reference in fiction. Suppose that the following sentence is true:

(4) The chief cyclops is identical with the strongest monster encountered by Odysseus

If we now substitute the "the strongest monster encountered by Odysseus" for "the chief cyclops" in (3a), we have

(3a3) In the *Odyssey* the strongest monster encountered by Odysseus lives in a cave

Statement (3a3), however, is very naturally taken as true; it
does accurately report the contents of the *Odyssey*. Substitution has preserved truth value. This instance represents
if not the universal case of such substitutions at least a
large class of them, and the conclusion must be that in
these instances this test of reference is passed. Even if one
can find cases where substitution does not preserve truth
value, this result does not affect those instances where it
does. So in a large class of cases this indicator gives a positive result for reference in sentences reporting the content
of a work of fiction.[33]

   In judging whether fiction passes the second test for reference, existential generalization, we must first deal with
the same question that arose with the theory of descriptions: does the existential quantifier appear inside or outside the scope of the operator? The most natural interpretation locates it inside, for the *Odyssey* is not to be taken as
making historical claims. This gives

(3a4) In the *Odyssey* there exists a chief cyclops and it lives in
a cave

33 Against an earlier version of this argument Robert Howell correctly
points out that there are substitutions not violating the conditions I gave
but which do not preserve truth value. See his "Fictional Objects: How
They Are and How They Aren't," p. 138. The present version accepts his
claim but, adopting for the sake of argument the tests of reference offered,
relies for its conclusion of reference in fiction on those cases where there
is substitution *salve veritate*. I might add that I do not offer this argument
in order to be able to deny that sentences reporting the contents of a work
of fiction can be prefixed by a fictional operator—the intention Howell
attributes to me—for of course I agree with him that such sentences are
subject to such an operator.

This is surely to be read as asserting that, among the creatures in the fictional world the Odyssey presents, there is a chief cyclops, one that lives in a cave. In other words, in the fictional situation depicted in the Odyssey there is a cyclops that exists, not one merely dreamed or hallucinated by Odysseus (which is why he turns out to be such a problem). And this is just what the Odyssey does say; existential generalization does not change truth value any more than substitution of coreferring expressions does. Fictional statements meet the two tests for reference; the claim that there is no reference in fiction has failed to find support.

There is a further class of cases for which the contention here, that references to fictions are under the scope of an operator and hence do not have reference, seems to have no plausibility whatever. These are cases (which in Chapter 4 I call "outside") for which there is no operator ranging over names and the like for fictions. I mean such instances as one already mentioned, "The chief cyclops is the most interesting monster in Greek literature." One cannot prefix this sentence with any operator of the sort we have been considering, and it is implausible to suppose that it can be analyzed in such a way that the definite description it includes appears under such an operator. The argument under consideration thus does not apply to these phrases and so does not offer a reason for denying them reference.

There are no doubt other ways of trying to implement Brentano's idea that expressions seeming to denote nonexistent objects can be paraphrased away. But I think that they encounter the problems above: either there is a conflict between the truth values of the initial sentences and their claimed paraphrases, or the paraphrases are about something other than what the initial sentences are about. If so, paraphrase is not available to deal with apparent designations of the nonexistent, and the proper account must respect the form these designations have as their actual and in some sense appropriate form.

2

REFERENCE AND FICTION

In this chapter I present a view of reference and apply it to
fictional discourse; it is important that I characterize at the
outset the notion of reference this view employs. Reference
in this sense corresponds very broadly to the everyday notion of "talking about." I say "corresponds" because I give
a description of the *practice* of talking about or referring, or
at least one central practice to which these notions apply—
one use, and I think clearly the most important use, of a
certain class of expressions. There may be other types of
act properly called "referring" but I do not consider them;
nor do I give an analysis of the ordinary meanings of "talk
about" or "refer." Nevertheless, the notion of reference I
employ is a familiar one in the philosophical literature and
quite distinct from its chief competitor, that appearing in
causal or historical connection theories, which attempt to
analyze reference in terms of some sort of realistic link between the entity referred to and the expression referring to
it. I comment on relations between these divergent views
of reference below. To present the conception I am adopting, it seems best to begin with a description of the particular use of expressions in the relevant class and then to
point out that on this conception there simply is reference
to fictions—to nonexistent objects. It is important to dis-
pute a rival view, that there is not genuine but only pre-

tended reference here, this leaves for the following chapter
the important matter of what kinds of objects fictions are.

REFERENCE AS IDENTIFICATION

Strawson has pointed out the particular use to which the relevant referring expressions are put:

Among the kinds of expressions which we, as speakers, use to make references to particulars are some of which a standard function is, in the circumstances of their use, to enable a hearer to identify the particular which is being referred to. Expressions of these kinds include some proper names, some pronouns, some descriptive phrases beginning with the definite article, and expressions compounded of these.[1]

Strawson calls such usages "identifying references" and this, or simply "references" for short, is the terminology I adopt. Another way of putting the idea is to say that an expression used in identifying reference forestalls the question, What (who, which one) are you talking about?[2] In identifying reference a speaker is singling out something for an audience through employing an expression used in accordance with the rules of language. It turns out that the relevant aspects of this situation are remarkably complex, and it is worthwhile trying to get clear about the elements in the standard situation where such an expression is employed. These seem to be the relevant ones:

1 P. F. Strawson, *Individuals: An Essay in Descriptive Metaphysics* (London: Methuen, 1959), p. 16. See also "On Referring," in *Logico-Linguistic Papers* (London: Methuen, 1971), p. 1, and "Critical Notice," *Mind* 71 (1962):252–254. See also John R. Searle, "Reference as a Speech Act," in *Speech Acts* (London: Cambridge University Press, 1978).

2 Strawson, "On Referring," p. 17.

(i) The speaker S has an object in mind and has the intention of directing the attention of the audience A to this object.

(ii) To carry out this intention, S utters (speaks, writes, etc.) in an appropriate context an expression whose standard function in the language is to execute such intentions.

(iii)S further intends that A recognize S's prior intention on the basis of this utterance.

When all these conditions are satisfied, S has made an identifying reference to an object x for A, or, more simply S has referred to x. The conditions could be further elaborated and additional ones given, but I believe that the above is sufficient for present purposes.

Such characterizations of speech acts have been much discussed and a number of comments are in order. First, the above account is meant to describe *one* standard use of expressions of the kind mentioned by Strawson. There may be others, for example, Donnellan has pointed out that there is a distinction between the "referential" and the "attributive" uses of definite descriptions, and perhaps they have other uses as well.[3] It is only the use in identifying reference that concerns me here. Second, the list above is intended to present the *characteristic* features of the situation in which referring expressions are used to identify. Simple description of a very familiar case is what is meant. The supposition is that any clearheaded individual can just recognize that these features are present in standard instances of referential use. For support of this claim I appeal to straightforward examination of unproblematic cases of the identifying use of names and descriptions; the list of conditions simply sets out what everyone can see is present there—so I hold. There is no need to give a priori argu-

3 Keith Donnellan, "Reference and Definite Descriptions," in *Readings in the Philosophy of Language*, ed. Jay F. Rosenberg and Charles Travis (Englewood Cliffs, N.J.: Prentice Hall, 1971), pp. 195–211.

ments or to rely on theoretical considerations such as "inference to the best explanation"—even if, as I suggest later, support of these sorts is in some measure available. Third, what is intended is the characterization of the *standard* or *typical* or *normal* case.[4] Nonstandard cases are certainly possible on this characterization and indeed are commonplace. An all-too-familiar instance is misremembering a name. If S says to A, "How is Mary?" where it is obvious to A that S means to be talking about A's current wife Joan, and where A has a ready explanation for the mistake in the fact that A's former wife was named Mary, the intended reference of "Mary" can go through (to Joan) despite the faux pas.[5] Donnellan's well-known example of "the man over there drinking a martini," where both speaker and hearer are under the mistaken expression that the man over there is drinking a martini and not sparkling water as he actually is, falls into this category as well.[6] Thus conditions (i–iii) are not meant as conditions for all cases reasonably classified as identifying reference but only of the standard case; counterexamples (such as Donnellan and Kripke give to descriptive theories of reference) do not

4 Searle puts the idea this way: "The proper approach, I suggest, is to examine those cases which constitute the center of variation of the concept of referring and then examine the borderline cases in the light of their similarities and differences from the paradigms"; *Speech Acts*, p. 28.

5 Given an appropriate psychological background, one might speak of a Freudian slip here; the faulty reference indicates that S disapproves of Joan and wishes that A were still married to Mary (as a possible scenario). So S is in some sense referring to Mary despite the surface intention to ask about Joan. Still, there is a clear sense in which S has made a mistake, and in any case not all such errors are plausibly explained as Freudian slips.

6 Keith Donnellan, "Reference and Definite Descriptions," p. 205. Saul Kripke gives a number of such cases in "Speaker's Reference and Semantic Reference," *Midwest Studies in Philosophy* 2 (1977):255–276. Kripke makes a distinction between speaker's reference, governed by a speaker's specific intention on a given occasion to refer to an object, and semantic reference, determined by the conventions of language (pp. 262–264). In what I am calling the standard case, these two types of reference coincide, but I make use of Kripke's distinction shortly.

themselves undermine the claim that (i–iii) give (at least some of) the features of normal identifying reference.[7] An account of nonstandard cases must be given in any full elaboration of this view of reference; happily, that is beyond the requirements of my project. Fourth, the mention in the list above of various kinds of intention calls to mind Grice's emphasis on this aspect of meaning.[8] What is useful in Grice's account is his emphasis on the element of the speaker's intention in the employment of a linguistic expression. One can regard the notion of reference presented above as combining Gricean concerns about speaker's intentions with Strawson's conception of reference as identification for an audience. Finally, there is a further condition of reference, the presence of an object referred to. This is a large topic and deserves its own discussion, to follow presently.

I want now to comment on the causal, or historical connection, theory of reference in view of its widespread popularity.[9] According to this theory, a proper name denotes its object because a historical or causal link has been established between name and object. Reference succeeds because of this existential connection between name and object rather than because the object is picked out by descriptions associated with the name. On one level, at least, this view need not conflict with the speech act view of reference given above. We can use Kripke's distinction be-

7 Thus disputing this view must rely on more than just finding cases of reference that violate the conditions set out. But I am not concerned here to defend this view of reference, only to present it.

8 H. P. Grice, "Meaning," *Philosophical Review* 66 (1957):377–388.

9 The contrast between an account of reference centering on the notion of "talking about" and the causal/historical theory has been discussed by Richard Rorty. See "Realism and Reference," *Monist* 59 (1976):324–327; *Philosophy and the Mirror of Nature* (Princeton, N.J.: Princeton University Press, 1980), p. 289; and "Is There a Problem about Fictional Discourse?" in *Consequences of Pragmatism* (Minneapolis: University of Minnesota Press, 1982), p. 127.

tween "semantic" and "speaker's" reference to clarify that
ters The semantic referent is what a speaker's words
designate; the speaker's referent is "the thing the speaker
referred to by the designator" whether or not it is the semantic referent.[10] If Kripke were to allow such a thing as a
standard instance of speaker's reference, I cannot see why
we would not have the characterization of reference I have
given. This characterization assumes that there is a paradigm situation for the use of the expressions in question
and intends to give the conditions satisfied there. So, if we
can suppose that for Kripke semantic and speaker's reference are both aspects of the referential situation, my account of reference emphasizes the speech act aspect while
leaving it open whether there is in addition always some
causal or historical connection between expression and object designated. Kripke evidently would not reject the phenomena I have listed as in some sense genuine aspects of
the referential situation, although he would not make
them central as they are in my account.

What can be said about this difference between speech
act and causal theories? I could recommend my view for
various reasons: there are various difficulties to which the
causal theory is subject,[11] and there are a priori attacks on
the theory itself.[12] I have considerable sympathy with these
objections. But it is less to the point here to engage in po-
lemics than to notice how the two accounts apply to fiction. It has been traditional for mainstream philosophers,

10 Kripke, "Speaker's Reference and Semantic Reference," p. 264. As
indicated (see n. 6), both types of reference coincide when the speaker's
beliefs about the object (and about the terms the speaker employs) are
true.
11 See, e.g., Gareth Evans, *The Varieties of Reference*, ed. John
McDowell (Oxford: Clarendon Press, 1982).
12 See Hilary Putnam, "Realism and Reason," in *Meaning and the
Moral Sciences* (Boston: Routledge and Kegan Paul, 1978), pp. 123–140,
and *Reason, Truth, and History* (Cambridge: Cambridge University Press,
1980).

perhaps under Russell's influence, to call names and descriptions in fiction and mythology "nondenoting," "nonreferential," "empty," and the like, on the ground that there is no real thing designated by them. Causal theorists would find this congenial, since obviously the use of a name for a fictional character cannot be accounted for by supposing that there is a historical individual baptized by the name and initiating a causal relation. Nevertheless, on the face of it such names constitute counterexamples to the causal theory: here are names in perfectly acceptable sentences which are not in any evident way causally related to a referent. So causal theorists have a particularly pressing reason for dealing with the nonexistence issue: their theory of reference seems to be at stake. Various proposals compatible with causal theory have been tried, but none of them work, or so I argue. And if they do not, this is a reason for favoring the approach I am offering. But the issue can be put in a less directly adversarial way—as a contest between two research projects, one incorporating a causal theory of reference, the other a speech act theory. So conceived, the two are to be evaluated on how well on the whole both account for the data, various facts about the language of fiction. I am not fond of looking at philosophical issues in this way, because it suggests that what philosophers should do is provide general principles applicable over broad ranges of fact and judged not by appropriateness to the particulars of a case but by other criteria, usually those of theory construction in the natural sciences. Details of fit to specific cases become less important than overall acceptability as determined by general theoretical considerations assumed to be relevant to explanations of any kind whatever. I do not believe that there are any such general considerations, and I am certainly not suggesting that the analysis of fictional discourse to follow should be judged on such a basis. Still, *if* one were to adopt this conception of method, then the account I offer would compare favorably with any incorporating the causal theory of reference—so I hold. Naturally this claim cannot be judged at this point; I am only asking for a fair hearing from those who adopt this methodology Indeed, insofar as this contention goes, I am only asking for the kind of hearing Parsons felt it was appropriate to request from his mainstream Russellian colleagues (see Chapter 1).

We can now return to the task of elaborating the account of reference begun earlier. If reference is a matter of identifying for an audience, then determining whether a particular expression is used referringly must take contextual features into account. Definite descriptions, expressions such as "the F" or "his F," are very often used referringly.[13] But not always: in "I did it for his sake" or "He left me in the lurch" they do not have this function. Searle explains that he knows this "because, as a native speaker, [he] can see that the utterances of [these definite descriptions] do not serve to pick out or identify some object or entity."[14] We might still want to know just how a native speaker sees this, how that speaker knows that these phrases are not meant to have this function; this is the question of how in understanding another's speech we understand intentions. One central indication is the standard use of an expession, since without reason to the contrary one is entitled to take a speaker as using a phrase according to its conventional employment. It is obvious that the definite descriptions in Searle's cases are embedded in idiomatic expressions where they do not have a referring use, for there is no particular sake or lurch being picked out for a hearer. It would show a misunderstanding to attempt further reference to some supposed lurch or sake, to wonder what properties they might have, or to try to count lurches or sakes. These

13 To simplify discussion, I consider only singular reference and not indefinite ("a book"), attributive ("somebody or other"), plural, or other cases.
14 Searle, *Speech Acts*, p. 73.

phrases are not to be brought into "interplay with the whole distinctively objectificatory apparatus of our language: articles and pronouns and the idioms of identity, plurality, and predication," as Quine puts it.[15] Similarly, the sentences above do not provide answers to questions such as, For what of his did I do it? and In what did he leave me?[16] The conception of reference I am proposing corresponds to a whole set of phenomena in the situation where referring phrases occur, including speaker's intentions, appropriateness of other denoting expressions, and the applicability of criteria of identity. To make a reference is to invoke this "whole objectificatory apparatus" and is not merely to employ an expression of a certain surface form—contrary to what Meinong would have held.

OBJECTS AND EXISTENCE

Reference is plainly always to an object. This is a conceptual requirement of the notion of reference, as is made clear in the account above (directing attention *to something,* answering, *What* are you talking *about?).* The critical issue of whether an object referred to must exist must eventually be addressed, but first I should discuss further the notion of an object—a notion of fundamental importance but one too often passed over without examination. To acknowledge something as a possible object of reference—a "referent," to adopt convenient terminology—is to grant that the "whole distinctively objectificatory apparatus of our language" applies to it, to repeat Quine's apt characterization. Something once referred to can be referred to again, perhaps through the use of a different ex-

15 Willard Van Orman Quine, *Word and Object* (Cambridge, Mass.: M.I.T. Press, 1960), p. 236.
16 Searle, *Speech Acts,* p. 73.

pression (e.g., a pronoun or a demonstrative instead of a name) There must in general be ways of tolling when the same object is present, when something differs from similar things, and how many such objects there are: for something to qualify as an object there must be associated with it criteria of identity and enumeration.[17] These conceptual facts about the notion of an object reflect the function that referring expressions have in identification. It is always logically appropriate for a hearer to ask a speaker for further specification of the intended referent, even if in response the speaker can only repeat in other terminology the content of the expression already employed. More broadly, the notions of *referring*, predicating an *attribute* of something, and the *truth* or *falsity* of the resulting *statement* are conceptually related.[18] On the view of language I want to put forward, there is a deep-level structure where the concept of an object plays a basic role. The various remarks above about objects I take to be conceptual truths indicating what is constituitive of this notion. That objects have (at least some) associated criteria of identity and enumeration and are bearers of properties, thus making them possible subjects of true/false (warranted/unwarranted) claims, are truths of this kind. This deep-level structure of our (or any) framework allows different purposes to be served, one of the principle ones being the communication of complex

17 It would be difficult and not especially worthwhile for present purposes to try to make this condition precise. Certainly there are vague predicates and hence indeterminate objects—waves, hills, puddles; see David Wiggins, "Indeterminate Particulars," in *Sameness and Substance* (Oxford: Basil Blackwell, 1980), pp. 205–206. The requirement of identity need not be so strict as to exclude all indeterminacy.

18 See my "Trancendental Arguments Revived," *Philosophical Investigations* 8 (1985):229–251. Quine's remarks in *Ontological Relativity and Other Essays* (New York: Columbia University Press, 1969,) pp. 8–9, are relevant here; see also Searle's discussions in *Speech Acts*. The classical treatment is Aristotle's *Categories*. I distinguish my views from these opinions below.

messages. Such communication is hardly to be accomplished without the possibility of a speaker's identifying an
object for an audience by referring to it—using with the
appropriate intentions in a suitable context a certain kind
of rule-governed expression. To repeat, these related conceptual facts (and perhaps others of a similar nature) are all
constituitive of the concept of an object of reference, which
thus is absolutely central to any conceptual scheme. Notice that this account has not included anything about existence; notably it has not implied that objects of thought or
reference must exist. Indeed, I believe that it is not part of
the notion of an object of thought or reference that it must
exist. This is of course a controversial claim and one I must
now spend some time justifying.

Whatever the differences dividing the philosophers mentioned above, there is agreement on the principle that all
referents exist. Quine remarks, "To be is to be in the range
of reference of a pronoun," or perhaps even more directly,
"Existence is what existential quantification expresses"; he
sees no divergence between something's satisfying the various linguistic criteria of pronominal reference, pluraliza-
tion, cross reference, and the like and that thing's existing.
Searle's first "axiom of reference" is "whatever is referred
to must exist."[19] This consensus illustrates what Meinong
called the philosophical "prejudice in favor of the actual"
and shows that this prejudice is not confined to Parson's
"orthodox tradition." Indeed, this is a view that has been
held throughout the entire history of Western philosophy.[20]

As is usual with long-standing prejudices, this one has

19 Willard Van Orman Quine, *From a Logical Point of View* (Cambridge: Mass.: Harvard University Press, 1953), p. 13; *Ontological Relativity*, p. 97; Searle, *Speech Acts*, p. 77.

20 A strong case can be made, I think, that this principle is not nearly
so widely held in Eastern thought. See Bimal K. Matilal, *Epistemology,
Logic, and Grammar in Indian Philosophical Analysis* (The Hague:
Mouton, 1961).

been noticed from time to time. The situation is so force-
fully and to my mind accurately expressed (in 1785!) by
that acute and stalwart defender of common thought,
Thomas Reid, that I cannot resist a rather lengthy quota-
tion:

> I am afraid that, to those who are unacquainted with the doc-
> trine of philosophers upon this subject, I shall appear in a very
> ridiculous light, for insisting upon a point so very evident, as
> that men may barely [simply] conceive things that never exis-
> ted. They will hardly believe, that any man in his wits ever
> doubted of it. Indeed, I know no truth more evident to the
> common sense and to the experience of mankind.[21]

Reid's view is that we can conceive (as opposed to perceive)
something that never did, does not, and never will exist,
"and that a bare conception of a thing does not so much as
afford a presumption of its existence."[22] His most relevant
case is that of a centaur: "The thing I conceive is a body of
a certain figure and colour, having life and spontaneous
motion."[23] Put in present terms, Reid's claim is that we can
refer to centaurs without assuming their existence in any
sense: "That centaur [in that story] is fierce" and "Those
centaurs are fierce" make perfectly good sense without any
presumption of centaurs' existence.

Perhaps it belabors the obvious to continue the point
that there is reference to the nonexistent, but in view of
the pivotal nature of the issue the matter must be made
absolutely clear. Let us consider the instance

---

21 Thomas Reid, *Essays on the Intellectual Powers of Man*, with an
introduction by Baruch A. Brody (Cambridge, Mass.: M.I.T. Press, 1969), p.
405.

22 Ibid., p. 409.

23 Ibid., pp. 419–420; Reid also considers universals (the circle), p. 422.
It is not quite clear whether it is some specific centaur (in a specific myth)
or centaurs in general that Reid is thinking of here; nothing in his remarks
precludes its being the former.

(1) Sherlock Holmes smokes a pipe

It seems quite natural to say of a suitable utterance of (1) that its speaker S in using "Sherlock Holmes" has something in mind which he or she wants to call to the attention of an audience A and is doing so by using a proper name, an expression that has the standard use of picking out the item of which it is the name. Now there is certainly something that S is talking about here, namely, the fictional detective in the famous stories. The sense of "there is" in which (1) is true is the subject of later discussion; it is important to note here only that it is perfectly appropriate according to everyday usage to say that (1) is true. There are criteria of identity for this character: Holmes in "The Hound of the Baskervilles" is the same character throughout and is identical to the protagonist of "The Sign of the Four"; he is different from the other figures in the Conan Doyle stories, Watson or Inspector Lestrade, for example, and is certainly to be distinguished from characters in a different series of tales, such as Hercule Poirot. The criteria of identity in effect for these perfectly obvious and straightforward remarks include considerations such as the following: certain names, descriptions, and pronominal references ("Sherlock Holmes," "the detective who lives at 221B Baker Street") found in the text of the stories are all naturally taken to concern the same character, for they are all meant to pick out the man who in the tales is of a certain height, weight, and facial description, and who lives at a certain place and has certain friends. In the story we apply exactly the same types of criteria for ascertaining that a single man is being referred to as we do in real life. It is certainly natural to take the author to be intending that we take these expressions as denoting a single character, since otherwise his writing becomes unintelligible. Not only are there in-text criteria, but the history of the writings is relevant: the stories including these names and descriptions were all originally published in *The Strand* between July 1891 and January 1905 and written by the same man, A. Conan Doyle. So there is no doubt that Holmes throughout is the same individual, distinguishable from other characters.[24] It is obvious the other conditions of reference apply. The appearance of "Sherlock Holmes" in (1) forestalls questions such as, Whom are you speaking about?; someone who did not hear the sentence clearly and asked the question could well find the repetition of the name a satisfactory reply. There are truths about Holmes [e.g., (1)] and falsehoods ("Holmes dislikes music"). On the other hand, it seems clear from the standpoint of history that Holmes is nonexistent:

(2) Sherlock Holmes did not exist

is certainly true and can be informative (e.g., to someone who hears talk about Holmes but is not familiar with the Conan Doyle series). And surely (1) and (2) have the same referent: the one who (in the stories) smokes a pipe, solves crimes, and is a friend of Watson is that very individual asserted by (2) not to exist—he is a fictional character created by Arthur Conan Doyle, as the explanation might continue. All of this seems perfectly straightforward and unproblematic; as Reid insisted, references to nonexistent objects are commonplace in ordinary discourse.

24 I do not want to suggest that there are never problems about the identity of figures in fiction or mythology. Students of comparative religion may find it controversial whether a figure appearing in one religion is the same as a figure appearing in another; one might wonder whether to call the youthful hero of the recent movie *The Young Sherlock Holmes* the same character as appears in the canonical Holmes writings. There is room for disagreement in such instances; such cases do not mean that identity is always undecidable. That identity is generally not an issue is a condition for the possibility of realistic fiction.

IS REFERENCE TO NONEXISTENT
OBJECTS ONLY PRETENDED?
SEARLE, WALTON, AND EVANS

The admission of reference to nonexistent objects marks a major divide in theories concerning nonexistence, and it is important to deal now with a popular rival opinion, that despite the data there is only pretended and not genuine reference to fictional characters. This is an attractive view for those wanting to "avoid Meinongian difficulties," for pretended reference is presumably not to a full-fledged object or perhaps to anything at all, and consequently the necessity of accepting nonexistent entities disappears. The question is whether this view can be supported given the facts of usage; I argue that it cannot. There are a number of ways of elaborating the basic pretense theme, and I do not deal with them all, but it is convenient to begin with Searle's version, for his views on reference have much in common with the position being developed here and it is important to make clear my differences with him. Searle remarks that the pretense here does not include an intention to deceive but is that in which one is engaging "in a performance which is *as if* one were doing or being the thing"—for instance, pretending to be Nixon in a game of charades.[25] This remark does not seem right, for on the face of it in telling a story one appears to be talking about its characters and not (usually, anyway) acting as if one were a character himself. Perhaps one could make the case that Conan Doyle was pretending to be Watson, yet many stories are not told from the viewpoint of a character but from some impersonal perspective. These remarks indicate a

---

25 John R. Searle, "The Logical Status of Fictional Discourse," in *Expression and Meaning: Studies in the Theory of Speech Acts* (Cambridge: Cambridge University Press, 1979), p. 65.

problem inherent in the pretence theory, that of providing a plausible account of just what the pretense is; this is a difficulty for the Walton–Evans version (discussed later in this section) as well. A second problem is that the theory does not fit the actual speech situation. Searle holds that there are "vertical rules" that correlate words or sentences to the world, for example, rules governing the applications of sentences in newspaper reports or history. Fiction, he continues, is not governed by such conventions; rather,

> what makes fiction possible, . . . is a set of extralinguistic, non-semantic conventions that break the connection between words and the world. . . . Think of the connections of fictional discourse as a set of horizontal conventions that break the connections established by the vertical rules. . . . In this sense, to use Wittgenstein's jargon, telling stories really is a separate language game; to be played it requires a separate set of conventions, though these conventions are not meaning rules.[26]

Problems for this view begin to appear with the attempt to explain various aspects of usage. Searle, we recall, adopts as an "axiom of reference" the principle that whatever is referred to must exist, and this principle appears above in the remark that the conventions governing fiction are nonsemantic and not meaning rules. It is this axiom that raises problems. An indication that something is wrong is the refusal to call conventions governing fiction meaning rules; what are they if not rules concerning meaning? Searle's difficulty is that for him meaning rules and semantics concern word–world relations and so cannot straightforwardly apply to fictional discourse; the linguistic regularities of fiction have to be called something else. This terminological awkwardness only foreshadows the real problems. Searle's view is that, although an author does not refer to

26 Ibid., pp. 66–67.

characters in writing a work of fiction (after all, antecedent
to the writing there are no such characters to refer to), once
the fiction is written "we who are standing outside the fictional story can really refer to a fictional person."[27] In such
a case as (1), for example, I "really referred to" a fictional
character (i.e., my utterance satisfies the rules of reference).
Searle is thinking of his axiom here; reference is always to
existent objects, either to what really exists or to what exists in fiction.[28] If, however, existence in fiction is to be
allowed as a kind of existence, then why are authors said
not to refer? Their utterances appear fully to satisfy Searle's
rules of reference. More serious than this internal matter is
the apparent commitment to two kinds of existence, historical and the kind fictional characters have, which is evidently something quite different.[29] This view could be
adopted (it has been attributed to Meinong), but it seems
unlikely that Searle wants it; if he does, why hold that fictional language breaks word world connections and deny
that there is a semantics of fiction? Certainly the view is
counterintuitive and needs motivation and defense; in its
absence one seems entitled to be doubtful about the proposal. The dual-existence theory raises questions about
other parts of Searle's view, for if word–world connections
are suspended in the writing of fiction, how can such writing subsequently result in things having a kind of existence
and allowing references that invoke word–world relations
again? Searle's theory introduces an undefended and un-
comfortable double existence and is subject to internal difficulties.

   A committed defender of the pretense view might feel
that Searle has just not been sufficiently thorough in his
denial of reference; it is not merely authors who should be

27 Ibid., pp. 71–72.
28 See *Speech Acts*, pp. 78–79.
29 This problem has been pointed out by Rorty, "Is There a Problem
about Fictional Discourse?" p. 118.

viewed as making pretended references but anyone using names and the like for fictional characters. The mixed nature of Searle's theory introduces the problems that a more consistent pretense account would avoid. This alternative brings us to the views of fiction originated by Kendall Walton and elaborated by Gareth Evans.[30] Much is admirable in this account; still, it fails to explain the use of referring expressions in fiction. Like Searle's it emphasizes that singular terms appearing in fiction are used rather than mentioned,[31] and it shows no sympathy with attempts at paraphrase. In this account it is noticed that there are language games of make-believe, typically originating in historical facts (as a game of mud pies originates with pats of mud) and entered into by adopting the pretense. Participants pretend to use singular terms in reference ("the two pies just out of the oven") but actually refer to the historical phenomena that generate the game (two mud pats and the old dresser drawer). By extensions of the game, players can introduce new truths ("I am going to eat my pie") or talk about features of the game not present at the game's start ("My pies are bigger than yours"). But whenever they use such expressions, players are operating under the pretense of the game and never actually referring; thus they never assume that there are nonexistent objects being talked about. This view transfers to literary fiction: "The initial

---

30 See particularly Kendall L. Walton, "Pictures and Make–believe," *Philosophical Review* 82 (1973):283–319, and "Fearing Fictions," *Journal of Philosophy* 75 (1978:5–27; and Gareth Evans, *Varieties of Reference*. I ignore the differences between their expositions, which are unimportant for our purposes. In *Mimesis as Make-Believe: On the Foundations of the Representational Arts* (Cambridge, Mass.: Harvard University Press, 1990), Walton has elaborated his theory and tried to deal with some of the issues I present. This book has appeared too late for me to be able to comment on this version of his views.

31 For example, "I take it to be obvious that in these cases [which include fiction] the singular term is *used* (albeit connivingly) and is not merely mentioned"; Evans, *Varieties of Reference*, p. 344.

pretense is that the novel (story, play, . . .) gives us information about things; but we know that further make-believe truths are generated by the initial pretense, and can
be reported in the same way."[32] So any use of a name for a
fictional character, whether in expressing alarm at what is
about to happen in a story ("Good grief—Holmes is about
to be shot!") or in dryly reporting contents ("Well, first
these people came to Holmes's office and told him the
problem; then the next day he went out to their country
house"), one is extending the story and still participating in
the make-believe, and so still merely pretending to refer.
The mixed character of Searle's theory is avoided and the
desired result gained that "there is no need to recognize
fictional objects, objects which have properties but lack existence."[33]

Let me note first that the explanation of pretending offered here is no more plausible than is Searle's. Is the author of a story "pretending to have knowledge of things and
episodes"?[34] As readers are we supposing for the moment
that a story "gives us information about things"? Someone
who did pretend to take the Holmes stories to be giving
information might show this by going to London and looking for Holmes's gravesite while only feigning the expectation of finding it, or by paging through the London newspapers of the 1890s simulating the outlook of someone
expecting reports of Holmes's exploits. Or suppose that
someone tells me a story about finding gold in the backyard.
If understanding a story is realizing that it is pretending to
give information, one way to show that I do understand is
to go into the backyard and start to dig—pretending that I
think I will find gold. These would be ways of carrying out
the pretense that a story gives information. Stories could be

32 Ibid., p. 366.
33 Walton, "Pictures and Make-believe," p. 287, n. 5.
34 Evans, *Varieties of Reference*, p. 353.

understood so as to make these consequences appropriate, but they are certainly not characteristic of the standard way of showing an understanding of fiction. Grabbing a shovel and heading for the backyard is hardly a reaction reflecting an understanding of a clearly made-up tale about gold and seems to indicate a misunderstanding—that it really was a factual account. If I explain by saying, "I'm pretending that there is gold there," I would be thought to be now engaging in my own act of pretense, not continuing the intentions of the storyteller.

A second consideration against the Walton-Evans version of the pretense theory is that stories can depict events that are physically and even logically impossible. Mythology has flying horses, the feats of comic book superheroes pay no attention to ordinary human limitations ("leaps tall buildings in a single bound"), and readers of science fiction do not blink at time travel. There is the curious tale of little Johnny with his round-square hoop, and the story of the man who squares the circle. On the face of it, it is quite implausible to take the authors of such tales to be pretending to have knowledge of such situations, for these are states of affairs that these authors might well hold to be impossible and so not knowable. Acknowledging that their stories are about objects or events that are genuinely impossible does not require authors to stop writing or render their speech unintelligible.

A third consideration is this. If authors are to be understood as the pretense theory proposes, then it is appropriate to ask them how they know the things they write about, what their evidence is. If they are pretending to know, then they should be willing to carry the charade further and say how they know. But to ask these questions and invite pretended evidence does not accord with the normal understanding of storytelling. Such questions would be taken as an indication of misunderstanding that it was a story being told. Standard epistemic considerations do not apply to storytellers who can deny that they have any knowledge or evidence without affecting the intelligibility of their performances.

There is a further objection to the Walton–Evans view. It was not gratuitous of Searle to hold that someone standing outside a story and reporting events occurring in a story is referring, for all the conditions of reference are met here: the user of the name of a figure in the fiction has something in mind to pick out for a hearer, and there is such a figure in the fiction. Unlike the storyteller, who is making it all up and not using language referentially (as Searle's advocate is willing to concede), the person outside the fictional situation is referring.[35] There is a real distinction between the use of singular terms by a storyteller and the use of such terms by people not caught up in the fiction but simply reporting the contents of the tale—a distinction ignored by the Walton–Evans account. The point is that, even if it is granted that some singular terms for fictions have pretended employments, it is not plausible to say this for all uses of such terms. This next case represents these issues:

(3) Sherlock Holmes was created by Arthur Conan Doyle

This statement should give Walton and Evans more difficulties than even a statement such as (2) ("Sherlock Holmes smokes a pipe"), which (according to Walton) asserts something that make-believedly is the case. After all, the content of (2) is at least part of a make-believe world, and there might seem to be some plausibility in holding that the references included in (2) take place within that

---

35 To exclude the case of the person who is participating in the game of make-believe and so (according to the Walton–Evans theory) only make-believedly asserting that p, let us be clear that our speaker here is genuinely asserting that make-believedly p. This distinction is made by Walton, "Fearing Fictions," p. 20.

world. But (3) offers no such possible analysis, for it asserts something not holding in any make-believe world; it is within the real world that Conan Doyle created Holmes. Walton cannot hold that (3) asserts a further truth generated by the pretenses of the novel, for Holmes's creation is not itself something that could be included in the world of the stories. So "outside" statements (as I call them in Chapter 4) stand as clear counterexamples to the Evans–Walton view that there is only reference within the pretense of the story.

Difficulties with the Walton–Evans proposals simply reinforce Searle's view that one can stand outside the fiction and make genuine references to fictional objects. My basic point is not to recommend Searle's version of the pretense view over that of Walton and Evans, for his is fatally flawed too. Rather, I am contending that pretense theories are just not acceptable. They must admit that there are *some* references to fictional objects [as in (3)] and admit further that references in fiction [e.g., (2)] are prima facie genuine with there being no plausible grounds for explaining them away as mere pretense. The reasonable view is that such references are not pretense at all.

3

THE UNREALITY OF FICTIONS

If fictional characters do not exist and yet are genuinely referred to, what kind of metaphysical standing do they have? Meinong is supposed, wrongly, to hold that the golden mountain and the round square have Being or subsistence, genuine reality although not the kind Mt. Everest or the equilateral triangle have. Is this the only possible position at this point? I think not; support can be given to something very much like Meinong's actual view that objects of reference have *so-sein* without having *sein*.[1] For illumination we must look closely at details of the language game of fiction and especially at the notion of the object of reference it incorporates. But before proceeding directly to this notion, I must say something about what might be called the structure of reference, a topic having much in common with issues discussed under headings such as "intentionality" or "intentional objects."[2] This done, I can proceed to distinguish these conclusions from those of

1 See "Solutions and Strategies" in Chapter 1.

2 These are relevant discussions: G. E. M. Anscombe, "The Intentionality of Sensation: A Grammatical Feature," in *The Collected Papers of G. E. M. Anscombe: Vol. II, Metaphysics and the Philosophy of Mind* (Minneapolis: University of Minnesota Press, 1981), pp. 3–20; and David W. Smith and Ronald M. McIntyre, *Husserl and Intentionality: A Study of Mind, Meaning, and Language* (Dordrecht, Holland: D. Reidel, 1982), pp. 40–61.

Meinong and other theorists, and to show how they meet objections.

OBJECTS AND THE STRUCTURE OF
REFERENCE

What I am calling the standard case of reference is that where the full set of intentions characteristic of reference is present, the relevant beliefs of speaker and hearer about each other and about the object, context, and relevant facts of language are true, and the speaker does indeed succeed in identifying the intended object through using an appropriate referring expression. Various aspects of this situation must be noted. First, I reemphasize that reference is always to something: it is a conceptual truth that a speaker intends to direct an audience's attention to an object. Without such an intention a speaker cannot be described as referring. But second, in this standard case two aspects of reference must be distinguished. On the one hand, there is the object qua referred to, the object as the speaker conceives it. When answering, What is the speaker talking about? in this sense, one mentions or describes the referent as the speaker believes it to be, using terminology suitably reflecting these beliefs. One might repeat the expression used by the speaker or employ locutions intended to capture this perspective. The speaker might be wrong about the properties of the thing spoken about; in fact, there might not even be any such thing. Nevertheless, What is the speaker talking about? could be appropriate as an inquiry into the speaker's conception of what he or she is doing. Anscombe calls the object in this sense the "intentional object."[3] On the other hand, one might describe the entity spoken about as it really is, without regard to a

3 Anscombe, "The Intentionality of Sensation," p. 3.

speaker's beliefs about it. Having understood what the speaker means to be talking about, one is not limited to terminology the speaker might employ but can use any descriptions deemed appropriate. For Anscombe this is the "material object." In Donnellan's case of the individual talking about someone at a party (see Chapter 2, n. 6) the intentional object is the man over there drinking a martini; the material object is the man over there drinking sparkling water. Anscombe's terminology is, however, inconvenient for my purposes, and I use "object in the absolute sense" or "absolute object" instead of her "material object."[4] This distinction is an important one and plays a central role in the forthcoming discussion. In the standard instance of reference, the intentional and the absolute (or "material") object correspond: the speaker knows what the object is like; the speaker's intentional object corresponds to the thing talked about. In all cases of reference there must be at least an intentional object, for a speaker must be thinking about something to intend to be identifying it for an audience. But there are various sorts of nonstandard case, ranging from those like Donnellan's, which includes an absolute object plausibly misunderstood, to the more

---

4 "Material object" suggests a commitment to physicalism (although Anscombe does not want to be so understood; ibid., p. 11), and to avoid this I employ the neutral "absolute object." It is important to preserve the contrast implied between her "material" and "intentional" objects. The latter is always relative to thought or reference (it is always an object *of* thought/reference); "material object" is not meant to be so relative (ibid., pp. 3–5). In common usage, "thing" and "entity" are nonrelative in this sense; "thing of thought" and "entity of thought" are solecisms. Still, "thing" and "entity" imply existence or at least belonging to the category of the existent (a notion I comment on later)—at any rate, this is a usage I follow throughout—and so do not suit my purposes. (But "something" is not limited to the existing; such are the vagaries of English!) I want to speak of something that is not relative to thought and yet that is possibly nonexistent; I claim that there is a category of objects that are simply nonexistent and yet not relative to thought. So I have devised the rather cumbersome "object in the absolute sense": something not relative to thought or reference and carrying no commitment as to existing or not.

extreme scenario in which a speaker is hallucinating and there simply is no appropriate object in the absolute sense I acknowledge such cases to be able to ignore them; I am concerned with standard cases only. Indeed, one of the points I mean to establish is that reference to a fiction can fully satisfy standard conditions; it is quite unlike the instance in which no absolute object corresponds to the intentional one. That is indeed a case where one might justifiably speak of a name as empty or nonreferring.

For there to be an instance of standard reference, an object in the absolute sense must be present in the framework shared by both speaker and audience. Communication requires shared beliefs, and within these the referent must be something both participants in the speech situation are prepared to acknowledge. The mode and degree of familiarity with the referent need not be the same; the speaker may be a specialist in a field of which the hearer has only the most elementary grasp, or the favored descriptions may be quite divergent. Still, there must be mutual acceptance of the item if the speaker is to bring it to the attention of the other, who in turn must understand himself as so led. A limiting case is that in which a speaker's use of a referring expression informs the hearer of the occurrence of the referent. Here the hearer must be willing to accept, on the basis of the speaker's presumed honesty, authority, or position to know, the speaker's implied belief that such a referent occurs. A second condition is that the speaker must be able to indicate the intended referent in such a way that the hearer can know which object is being picked out. This will typically be through the use of a suitable referring expression, but other linguistic means and even nonlinguistic ones are sometimes available, for example, pointing or signaling. The hearer must understand the expressions or devices used and the conventions governing them. In summary, in paradigm cases of communication (and hence reference) speaker and auditor must share a set of views about the world including beliefs about what kinds of object there are. Both must accept conventions governing linguistic or other devices used in reference, and in a given situation both must grasp that the speaker is actually employing one of these devices to pick out a particular object. Speaker and hearer must share a framework of common factual beliefs, commitments to entities, and conventions. These comments describe the relationship between fundamental elements in the speech situation: objects and knowledge of them by speakers and hearers, intentions that characterize acts of communication and understanding, and linguistic and other devices used to perform these acts. These remarks are conceptual in that they set out the content of the notions in question: the concepts of an object, of reference, of understanding a statement.

FRAMEWORKS AND TYPES OF OBJECT

Our framework is constituted by beliefs about various types of object adopted in response to a variety of needs and interests.[5] To put matters this way is not to deny that things of various kinds exist; rather, it is to regard things from the standpoint of the concepts we must use in thinking about them. There are various families of terms available for speaking about these different types of entity, and associated with the employment of this vocabulary are more or less distinct practices used in testing claims about objects of a given type. The farmer keeps a close eye on his

5 "Our framework" here refers to the beliefs, commitments, and rules accepted by mature and well-educated Westerners. There is, I hold, a conceptual core that all frameworks must share, but fictional discourse is not part of the contents of this core and consequently the status of fictional entities may vary from one scheme to another—a possibility to be looked at later. Still, it is reasonable to suppose that all cultures have a conceptual stratum counterpart to the one I am mining in this study.

orchards, pruning his trees, watering and giving fertilizer as he sees fit, and on the basis of his experience judging when to pick his apples. He is actively involved over long periods of time with his plants and their products. The mathematician leads a quite different life. Unlike the farmer's, her objects are entirely abstract, not being open to empirical testing or physical manipulation, and consequently her procedures involve such processes as adding and multiplying in her head, entering figures into a computer and reading the results, speaking with her colleagues about mathematical problems, and consulting mathematical journals and texts. The chess master operates with yet another set of items—pieces on a board whose moves and goals are defined by the rules of a game. His characteristic procedures are calculation of possible game variations while sitting at a chess board in a chess tournament, studying openings on his home chessboard, analyzing with his fellow masters, and proposing opening innovations to be tested by tournament play. The farmer, the mathematician, and the chess master share beliefs about ordinary reality and have a common (or at least intertranslatable) vocabulary for describing it. Still, each possesses in an especially high degree a mastery of the terminology and practices suitable to his or her own particular activity. Within a shared framework each is especially expert at his or her own language game. Procedures appropriate for deciding claims in these three areas are quite distinctive. The farmer could not employ only the mathematician's techniques of sheer calculation in dealing with his apples—he has to pick them, box them, make cider out of some of them—and the procedures of the chess master are even more irrelevant to him. Nor could the mathematician or the chess master make any use of the techniques of farming. And while the activities of the chess player involve calculations over abstractions, they take place in a setting entirely different from the mathematician's. One can think of our framework as consisting of a conceptual core generated by human faculties of perception, manipulation, and movement and by our interests and needs, with various more specialized conceptual strata with their subject matters and associated practices developing around this core and presupposing it.

At the center of this framework are commonsense things—everyday items, other human beings and animals, the familiar world. Indeed these entities could not be denied philosophically without incoherence.[6] But beliefs about other objects vary: there are societies in which advanced mathematics is unheard of, for example, and even in sophisticated cultures individuals disagree on religious figures, occult entities, and controversial topics such as the Loch Ness monster or ghosts or souls. Our framework is not monolithic; there are many classifications of object— many types of object in the absolute sense—accepted within this scheme. Commonsense physical objects, numbers, and moves in a board game are in some clear sense different types of thing but are all acknowledged by mature and sophisticated people. It would be a large undertaking to try to catalogue the various categories of object (in the absolute sense) accepted in this scheme; perhaps Meinong's theory of objects had this as a goal. I am merely pointing out that our framework does accept many kinds of object without being concerned here with matters of justification or relation to "ultimate" reality; my task is descriptive only. But among the accepted categories of object, fictions occupy their own conceptual stratum.

FICTIONS AS A CONCEPTUAL TYPE

My claim is that fictional objects as embedded in literary discourse constitute a distinct conceptual type. They are

6 See my "Transcendental Arguments Revived," *Philosophical Investigations* 8 (1985):229–251, for this argument and for further comments on our general conceptual framework.

accepted by our culture in the sense in which I have just noted that society, adding to a presupposed conceptual core, may recognize specialized types of objects reflecting particular interests and associated with appropriate vocab ulary and practices. To demonstrate this, I must recall obvious facts about fictional discourse. First, there need not have been any such thing. We can conceive a society that simply does not have the concept of a fictional character. In such a society language might be used to recount history, discuss practical affairs, state theories in physics, speculate about the future—but in this society it would not be possible to tell stories or myths or to write novels. Uses of language would be entirely literal; any attempt to describe individuals in imaginary situations would be met with misunderstanding and perhaps the charge of lying. Indeed something like this has been claimed, perhaps with doubtful accuracy, of mountaineers in the American South. Of someone who had written fiction about such mountaineers,

> the mountain boys were ready to mob him. They had no comprehension of the nature of fiction. [His] stories were either true or false. If they were true, then he was "no gentleman" for telling all the family affairs of people who had entertained him with their best. If they were not true, then, of course, they were libellous upon the mountain people.[7]

The author of these remarks believed, rightly or wrongly, that a certain group simply lacked the concept of fiction. These individuals held that talk about people was either true to the historical facts or was false of them; there was no such thing as speaking about an imaginary situation in which there are fictional characters based on real individuals.

7 Quoted by Horace Kephart, *Our Southern Highlanders* (New York: Macmillan, 1913), p. 208.

What are the rules of this dispensable language game? One of them is that someone can introduce a character into a story simply by writing certain kinds of sentences containing proper names and other singular terms. In children's literature this is sometimes signaled by a conventional phrase such as "once upon a time there was . . . . " In sophisticated fiction typically there are just sentences including referring expressions. A character so introduced might be given certain explicit features of body, personality, dress, and so on through the range of normal human traits. He or she might be described as having a history and said to have thoughts and emotions and the ability to to make decisions; these result in a series of events in which the characters have a part. All of these elements occur against a background situation that provides a setting for the occurrences in the story. A knowledgeable reader understands that an author using language in these ways is (as we say) *creating* a set of characters in the course of writing a story. It is understood that these characters do not exist—at least they do not considered as characters in a story (stories can be written about real people, a complication I discuss later). A reader realizes that a figure in one story can reappear in another and knows how to tell when two characters are the same over a series of tales. The criteria employed are simply the names and descriptions occurring in the various stories and perhaps relevant social and historical considerations.

It is also part of the language game of fiction that readers are licensed by expressions in the text of a fictional work themselves to make references to the characters and occurrences in stories. Such references occur in such activities as describing these characters and events, expressing judgments about them, or comparing them with characters in the same and other fictions. These reports, judgments, and comparisons can be correct or incorrect and are tested by consulting stories' contents—by reading them or asking someone who has, or by consulting summaries. These are just some of the features of the conceptual regularities in force for fiction; I have simply recalled familiar facts about uses of language concerning fiction, and in Chapter 4 I comment extensively on the linguistic employments alluded to here. These reminders are not intended to be controversial, and the expectation is that everyone agree to them. Taken together (along with other such points) they describe the linguistic practice of fictional discourse: they reflect the interwoven set of rules, vocabulary, and practices making up this language game. In so doing they show the conceptual station literary fictions occupy.

The distinctiveness of the logical facts about fictional discourse indicates that literary fictions (and mutatis mutandis imaginary items generally) constitute a special type of object in the absolute sense. Fictional characters and events are subjects for our interest and discussion which we do not find in the world as we find rocks, birds, other human beings, or even electrons and viruses, but which we create by the procedures of storytelling. Fictions are *unreal*, conceptual objects creating by using language in the ways practiced by authors and storytellers. These objects do not belong to the category of the real and contingently nonexistent (as for example do deceased historical individuals)—a point I elaborate shortly. If someone were to apply the procedures characteristic of interest in historical figures to Sherlock Holmes, this would indicate an error in classification; indeed, this is the sort of error pretense theorists make (see Chapter 2). Methods appropriate to discovering facts about Holmes are such straightforward techniques as reading the stories in which he appears or asking other readers about them. There is no such thing as finding out about Holmes by consulting histories of Victorian London, looking through the newspapers of that era, trying to locate his letters or personal belongings, searching for his relatives, or visiting the place where he lived.[8] When we give the conceptual category to which Holmes belongs, we say that he is a fictional character. This statement locates this object in the same way that "an apple is a fruit" or "seven is a number" locates objects. In such descriptions, items are being given their absolute classification, the conceptual type to which they belong. Literary fictions constitute a distinct category of object accepted by our conceptual framework.

FICTIONS AS UNREAL

Common discourse is quite clear on the nonexistence of fictions; "fictional characters do not exist" is a logical truth of a kind with "bachelors are unmarried," and if the common conception of fictions is faithfully to be set out this truth must be preserved. Indeed the kind of nonexistence fictions enjoy must be made clear. Let me approach this by remarking that I am speaking about the absolute classification fictions have qua fictions. From this standpoint Sherlock Holmes is nonexistent: "He did not really exist," we might explain; "He is only a character in some stories." Yet there is another perspective, that of a participant in the situation a literary work sets out: Watson

8 Holmes enthusiasts who have decorated flats according to the descriptions in Conan Doyle's writings realize (if they are not completely mad) that they are constructing a physical situation corresponding to Conan Doyle's descriptions; they do not believe that they are preserving the actual effects of the great detective in the way that Dickens's house and effects have been preserved in Bloomsbury. I myself have walked along Baker Street and was disheartened to find 221 the present site of a large and impersonal financial institution lacking any notice of the setting of the famous stories. I took this as a failure of sensitivity to literature rather than the desecration of a historic site. One the other hand, the hotel nearby on Baker Street advertising "Mrs. Hudson's Afternoon Teas" acknowledges the fiction while exploiting it commercially.

would find Holmes real and existing. These are matters to
be explored in the next chapter, or prevent I want only to
make it clear that it is the absolute classification of
Holmes—what kind of object he is from the logical standpoint of individuals logically outside the fictional world—
which is of present concern. Just what is the conceptual
type "fictional character"?

Meinong's conception exactly fits literary fictions, I believe: they have *so-sein* without having *sein*. They are
items to be spoken about and conceived as having properties, but they have no type or degree of existence whatever—they are *Aussersein*. My task is to make it convinc-
ing that this Meinongian category is appropriate for the
common conception of a fiction, for there is certainly a
strong inclination to think that whatever can be talked
about and have properties must be there, existing somehow. Let me begin by showing that the notion of an object
with *so-sein* without *sein* appears in other contexts. For
this I rely on Anscombe's analysis of the concept of the
direct object of a sentence. Consider her example "John
sent Mary a book." The direct object of this sentence is a
book according to an older usage, says Anscombe. Later usage puts this differently, calling the direct object the phrase
"a book," but each way of describing the situation is acceptable. It is the older parlance that is interesting for present purposes, and what the possibility of such usage
shows is that in the concept of a direct object there is the
concept of something we can talk about and make statements about, but for which the question of existence does
not arise. Anscombe points out that "it is evident nonsense
to ask about the mode of existence or ontological status of
the direct object as such."[9] Anyone grasping the grammatical notion of a direct object understands that a direct object
is given by a phrase standing in a certain relation to the

9 Anscombe, "The Intentionality of Sensation," p. 11.

verb. What we call a direct object is something generated entirely by the production of a sentence; it has nothing to do with whatever the sentence is intended to assert or whether the sentence is true. There may not be any entity corresponding to the phrase indicating the direct object; this has no bearing on the fact that something is a direct object. A direct object is introduced purely through the production of a grammatically acceptable sentence of a certain kind, and grammatical considerations alone, not reality, determine what is a direct object. Here we have just what Meinong called attention to, objects of thought and judgment lacking *sein*.

This phenomenon of the grammatical introduction of objects occurs on a much larger and more elaborate scale in the composition of literary works: fictional characters are also introduced entirely through a grammatical movement, through the construction of sentences by authors in the course of writing novels and stories. Like direct objects, fictions are purely intentional, having no status in existence at all. Nevertheless, having been generated by being written about in this way, they are appropriately referred to and made the subject of truth-valued claims.[10] Fictional characters have, from the standpoint of their conceptual station in our framework, no rating at all on a reality scale, not even a low one or one giving them the abstract status of Being or subsistence. There are such objects solely in the sense that they have been written about and thereby become available for thought or reference. It is convenient to introduce a technical term for items having this standing analogous to Anscombe's "intentional object": I call them "mere referents" or "conceptual" or "grammatical" ob-

10 This is apparently not Anscombe's view: names for fictions are "vacuous"; "['Mr. Pickwick' and 'Zeus'] name no man and no god, since they name a fictitious man and a false god" (ibid., p. 5). But Anscombe says so little about literary and mythical fictions that it would be wrong to put too much weight on her few remarks about them.

jects." So we can add that by much things as "There are seven characters in that story," where "there are" asserts not existence but the occurrence of certain grammatical objects. The chief criteria for the occurrence and identity of such items are what I have emphasized previously: the appearance in the relevant tales of names, descriptions, and the like taken to refer to a set of characters. Of course stories are made up of more than just characters; there is a whole world of persons and events against a background often taken over from history. This intentional world is created by an author just by writing under the conventions governing fictional discourse, for there is no reason why complex situations (and not just individual objects) should not be brought about entirely by grammatical means. But such a world and its contents are purely grammatical, constituted by items whose entire status is to be available for reference and thought and having no existence at all.

In common thought such contents are given a special station distinct from things that are factually nonexistent through destruction or having become extinct. We say that they are "unreal" or "imaginary" or "fictitious."[12] Holmes does not exist, but unlike empirically nonexistent people who have yet to be born or who have already died, he is unreal. Gladstone was a real man although he no longer lives; Holmes is fictitious and thus unreal and so never did exist. Dodos are real but extinct; unicorns are mythical and never had the genuinely historical status dodos enjoy. Thus

11 Intentional objects are objects *of thought*, items qua thought about; grammatical objects are objects *of reference*, items qua referred to. An intentional object can fail to be a grammatical one through there failing to be a sentence about it. But all mere referents are intentional objects, for reference includes thinking of the intended referent.

12 Gareth Evans rightly remarks that "the concept 'is real' is very different from the concept 'exists'"; *Varieties of Reference*, p. 352. But beyond this we disagree on how "unreal" is to be analyzed, a difference too ramified to be explored here (see his discussions, pp. 353, 369–372).

unicorns are not extinct, but this is a logical not an empirical fact; it was never open to them to become extinct. The categories of the contingently nonexistent and the unreal have associated with them different procedures. Real but nonexistent things arc found to be so by empirical investigation; no doubt expeditions and repeated studies were needed to ascertain that dodos had indeed become extinct. Gladstone's death was a matter of historical record. On the other hand, it would reflect a misconception to travel to distant continents to locate the habitats of unicorns and find evidence of their dying out; they are firmly classified as mythical and so can be learned about solely through study of the appropriate myths. Holmes's nonexistence could not have been a matter of empirical discovery, since he is a literary creation. Being unreal and being real but not existing historically are quite different classifications explained in terms of different types of consideration: the former is a purely grammatical or mental category having to do with the acceptance of certain linguistic practices or with acts of the imagination; the latter is a factual classification requiring the procedures characteristic of empirical investigation. The present study takes as its subject matter unreality, not empirical nonexistence.

The general analysis I have given here goes against mainstream opinion, since as Reid pointed out long ago the principle that whatever can be spoken of exists is deeply embedded in Western philosophical thought—a principle Meinong more bluntly called a prejudice. I want to support the analysis above by showing how its implications fit the details of practices characteristic of fiction. This means going more closely over ground already surveyed, but in view of the controversial nature of the issue I believe that this is called for. An author creates a character simply by writing out sentences that include proper names, descriptions, pronouns, and similar terms. Characters can then be

read about, discussed and compared with other characters,
and become the subject of evaluations, emotional reactions, and critical and historical studies. In this way fictions become public objects, available to the investigation
of anyone interested. Such acts of creation and such characteristic responoeo on the part of readers and critics all center around language. An author has merely written out sentences read by others with the understanding tht they set
out a story and thus license further sentences expressing
the kinds of activities noted. Such assertions can be veri-
fied by returning to the contents of a story—reading it or
consulting someone who has—and noting whether the
contents of the story are as claimed. All these acts are essentially conceptual and do not require recourse to anything nonlinguistic. Such activities as creating a character,
comparing one with another, checking claims about characters and fictional events—all involve simply writing,
reading, consulting accounts of texts, and the like. They
make no appeal to recognizable entities independent of discourse. There are sometimes apparent counterexamples;
one might say, "I saw Sherlock Holmes today," but this
would mean, for example, that one saw an actor dressed
like Holmes or someone masquerading as Holmes (similarly, "I saw Santa Claus in a department store"). Sentences apparently comparing real and fictional characters
are also possible: "Sherlock Holmes is more intelligent
than I am," someone might remark. But one looks to reality for information about the real individual only; for information about the character one consults stories.

If I am right and the practices falling under the language
game of fiction are ones carried out solely within a linguistic context, then it is gratuitous to hold that references in
fiction must be to extralinguistic entities having some sort
of existence or Being. There is nothing in the actual practice of the language game of fictional discourse to support
such a claim. One simply learns to use names of characters

referentially in learning to understand novels and to take it that what one is then talking about is a purely grammatical object—something not to be understood as having any sort of reality whatever. It is not part of the teaching process to indicate to a learner that there is a kind of reality apart from what familiarly exists (Being, subsistence) and which is being denoted by names and other referring expressions taken from fictional works. A philosophically committed theorist who claimed this (i.e., "The name 'Sherlock Holmes' is not only used in the way usual for literary fictions but in addition denotes something having the metaphysical status of subsistence where Holmes actually occurs") would completely mystify a learner and make no contribution to his or her mastery of fictional discourse. It is simply a fact that human beings have the capacity to write and understand certain sentences including referring expressions, and to make references on this basis, where these referents do not have any sort of existence whatever. Fictional discourse has no grounding in any further metaphysical reality; this linguistic practice itself and not some independent ontological realm is the fundamental fact in any account of the status of fictional characters. Here Wittgenstein's observation seems entirely appropriate: "Our mistake is to look for an explanation where we ought to look at what happens as a 'proto-phenomenon'. That is, where we ought to have said: *this language-game is played*."[13] This is not all there is to say about the matter, however, for one might still wonder how there could ever come to be a language game that included reference and prediction to the nonexistent—a topic broached in the next chapter. First I must deal with an opinion that apparently makes just the claim I do about the status of fictions—and then there are objections to be disposed of.

13 Ludwig Wittgenstein, *Philosophical Investigations*, 3rd ed. (New York: Macmillan, 1958), §654.

KRIPKE ON FICTIONS AS NONEXISTENT

Saul Kripke has views that might appear similar to those just expounded. "No counterfactual situation is properly describable as one in which there would have been unicorns," and similarly, "Granted that there is no Sherlock Holmes, one cannot say of any possible person that he *would have been* Sherlock Holmes, had he existed."[14] The problem with claiming that unicorns might exist, according to Kripke, is that unicorn myths do not specify the internal structure of unicorns, and internal structure is what identifies members of a species. So given various distinct hypothetical species each having the external appearance of a unicorn but different internal structures, we cannot say which of these species would have been the unicorns. Kripke does not explain as fully the problem with saying that Holmes might have existed, but if it is parallel to the one for unicorns it would be that the Holmes stories do not specify the conditions for identifying an individual as Holmes.[15] Since various possible or even actual people might have performed Holmes's exploits, there is no way of saying which one is Holmes.[16] This I believe is Kripke's reasoning; his account here is admittedly sketchy, and my presentation of his views should be taken as tentative.

If I have correctly reported Kripke's thinking, then his conclusion about the impossibility for individual characters to exist agrees with mine but for reasons I cannot accept. On my view a character is grammatical and is created by an author by writing a text, a procedure that cannot produce a real person. There could be a person on whom the Holmes stories are *based*, but this would not be the fic-

14 Saul Kripke, *Naming and Necessity* (Cambridge, Mass.: Harvard University Press, 1980), pp. 156–158.

15 Kripke views the origins of an individual as essential to it; ibid., pp. 110–115.

16 Ibid., pp. 156–158.

tional character itself—a matter elaborated in Chapter 6. No matter what is said in the stories about Holmes, even about his parents, Holmes could not exist. It is not that we lack a way of identifying the real Holmes, but that there could be no such way, for the supposition that Holmes could exist is mistaken: Holmes's absolute category does not permit existence. Kripke, however, seems to allow that there are circumstances in which we might identify a real person with the character: if the stories specified Holmes's parents and we found a real individual having these parents and having Holmes's characteristics and doing his deeds, then that individual would be Holmes. This I cannot accept; Holmes is a grammatical object and so cannot exist, a point argued above and developed further in Chapter 4.

The problem of fictional species is a different one. It seems to me that, in general, we do not take species as necessarily fictitious or mythical or imaginary; something falling under a general kind term could, qua member of a kind, appear in fiction, myth, or reality. So there could be real horses and unreal ones, real unicorns and unreal ones. Real unicorns could have evolved as a species and individual unicorns would have been born in the usual biological way, unlike fictional unicorns created by the imagination. In claiming this, I assume that we have a way of identifying members of the species, and here I take issue with Kripke's view that it is internal structure that identifies such members. Arguing this would require discussions having little to do with fiction and so are out of place here. Still, if I am right, then Kripke is mistaken in holding that there cannot be real unicorns. The only way I could agree with Kripke's view here is with the reading that unicorns just are unreal creatures—that it is part of the concept of a unicorn that it is unreal, in the way that it is part of the concept of a fictional character that it is unreal. I doubt that this reading could be maintained; there seems to be nothing obviously logically wrong with the claim that uni-

corns have been found in a remote part of Scotland, as
there certainly would be in the remark that fictional characters have been found there. Perhaps it is arguable that
some types of object are inherently unreal (centaurs!—and
this seems certainly so for round squares). But suppose that
it could be argued that unicorns are inherently unreal. Then
no matter what was said about the identity conditions for
unicorns, they could not exist; even if myths gave the internal structure of unicorns, we could not say of any real
thing that it was a unicorn. This position would disagree
with Kripke's; under these circumstances we could identify
real things as unicorns (if I read him correctly). So, on the
only condition under which I could agree with Kripke's
view that unicorns could not exist, I must reject his reason
for this view as incompatible with this condition.

These are clear differences between my account and
Kripke's, but I suspect that the basic difference is that I
acknowledge a category of the unreal while Kripke does
not. My suspicion is based on what he has published and
on his lectures, but a final evaluation must wait for the
publication of his promised book.[17] I should mention that,
from what I do understand of Kripke's account of the conceptual status of fictional characters, I believe that certain
objections I have offered to other proposals apply to his as
well; see particularly the critique of van Inwagen's account
in Chapter 5.[18]

OBJECTIONS AND REPLIES

A number of objections might be made at this point, and
each deserves a reply. The first concerns the topic of nega-

17 Ibid., p. 158.
18 For comments on Kripke's views on fiction, see Robert Howell, "Fictional Objects: How They Are and How They Aren't," Poetics 8 (1979),
and Evans, Varieties of Reference, pp. 367–368.

tive existentials. On the account above, a statement such as

(1) Sherlock Holmes did not exist

refers to a fictional character and simply says of him that he did not exist. We do have occasion to make such remarks; to a listener who heard a conversation but was unfamiliar with the stories, one might say "Holmes did not exist. He was a fictional character," thus indicating Holmes's conceptual status as a mere referent. I have considerably more to say about this in Chapter 4, but for now let me deal with the objection that my account commits me to a wrong analysis of such statements. There are paraphrases that show that there is no reference to nonexistent objects, not even to "merely grammatical" ones. Although this contention is in the spirit of paraphrase strategy rejected in Chapter 1, objections made there to it do not consider precisely negative existentials. So it might seem that I have not refuted the suggestion that negative existentials can be paraphrased so as to eliminate reference to nonexistent objects. One such suggestion[19] is that the meaning of (1) is given by

(2) Nothing has all the properties ascribed in the story to Sherlock Holmes

Statement (2) means that nothing real has all Holmes's qualities; it does not mean that nothing fictional does, for after all Holmes has all Holmes's qualities. But (2) so interpreted does not capture the meaning of (1). For suppose, miraculously, that there were a real person with all the

19 Such a suggestion is made (albeit somewhat tentatively) by Peter van Inwagen, "Creatures of Fiction," *American Philosophical Quarterly* 14 (1977):308 n. 11. I discuss his general theory of fiction at length in Chapter 5.

properties ascribed in the story to Holmes. This fact would not falsify (1), for even given the miracle, the fictional character created by Conan Doyle in his famous detective stories does not exist. A story is not about anything real even if, amazingly, there are real events that exactly correspond to it; hence the denial of the existence of a character is not the denial of anything real. Statement (1) acknowledges the occurrence of something that does not belong to the category of the real: there is something that can be talked about but not under the conventions of historical discourse. So this try at a paraphrase will not do.[20] It is difficult to think of other plausible candidates. In view of this, the failure of (2), and the unsoundness of paraphrase theories generally, we seem required to conclude that there are no ways of interpreting negative existentials concerning fictional characters so as to avoid reference to nonexistent objects.

A second group of objections is raised by Quine, who is concerned to rebut the notion that there are unactualized possibles which, although they do not exist, nevertheless have that lower form of actuality, subsistence. This is not the position that I claim ordinary thought grants to literary fictions, since these are not *possibilia* and further they do not have subsistence but merely conceptual status. Still, it may be illuminating to deal with Quine's worries. The specific position he is considering admits unactualized possibles and thus is committed to an "overpopulated universe [that] is in many ways unlovely" and "offends the aesthetic sense of us who have a taste for desert landscapes." But worse, it has no principled way of answering questions such as, How many possible fat men in the doorway are

20 Van Inwagen (ibid.) also mentions as a possible paraphrase "There is no such man as Sherlock Holmes." He takes this as having the same meaning as (2), in fact as being more precisely expressed by (2). This attempt is, however, subject to the same difficulties as (2): the existence of a real man with Holmes's qualities would not falsify (2).

there? and Are they identical to the possible thin men in the doorway?[21] These may be telling objections against the view Quine is opposing—one often wrongly ascribed to Meinong—but they have no force against the analysis presented above. For according to the latter, something is a fictional character only if an author more or less explicitly puts it into some work of fiction; nothing can become the kind of nonexistent object this study concerns unless it is created to be such. Simply inventing a name or a description does not thereby produce a fictional character, for a character is available as a referent only if it has been knowingly created to appear in a fictional situation, this typically being accomplished through writing out stories with the understanding that fiction is being composed.[22] So there is not an indefinitely large number of fictions out there awaiting reference; there are only the characters and other items actually created and explicitly introduced into stories by their authors.

Quine is worried not only about numbers but also about identity, but again I can deal with the problem by taking account of criteria present in actual practice. Usually we can count individuals constituting the cast of a given literary work. As a rule there is no difficulty in telling when a character is identical with a previously occurring one; a story would be incoherent if this were not generally the case. There can be works where it is unclear, perhaps intentionally so, how many characters there are or when one is the same as another. These are exceptions, and here the exceptions prove the rule: we would not find these cases

21 Willard Van Orman Quine, "On What There Is," in *From a Logical Point of View* (Cambridge, Mass.: Harvard University Press, 1953), p. 4.

22 Writing a story is perhaps the most formal procedure for introducing a character; this is done less formally by, for example, making up bedtime stories or telling a joke. Or an author might simply think up a character before putting him into a novel. For such instances, it seems natural to say that there are conventions corresponding to those employed by an author and having their logical features.

unusual unless typically there were no problem of determining identity It is precisely by omitting or obscuring
normal criteria of identity that an author can make a question of "same character." unclear. Quine's questions are
answered by appeal to criteria found in everyday practices
concerning fiction.

IS ORDINARY THOUGHT MEINONGIAN?

I should like to end this chapter with comments on the
relation between the principles I claim constitute the rules
for common fictional discourse and the opinions of
Meinong. Any discussion of this bold and ground-breaking
philosopher must deal with the fact that his views have
been distorted by those who took themselves to be dis-
agreeing with him. Meinong has usually been thought to
advocate the position contested by Quine above—that nonexistent objects merely subsist and do not fully exist. As I
have pointed out, this is not Meinong's view, which separates the occurrence of property-bearing objects from their
existence: *so-sein* is independent of *sein*. In what follows,
this clarification must be kept in mind.

Meinong and common practice accept that any genuine
reference requires an object even where the designata do
not exist. This position separates them from paraphrase
and pretense views, which have until recently dominated
the thinking of professional philosophers. Further, Meinong and ordinary practice agree with the principle that an
object can have properties without existing in any sense.
However, as I have pointed out, there is a major difference
in what counts as reference. Common fictional discourse
accepts reference only where it occurs within the context
of an ordinary speech situation, and so the test of reference
cannot be purely syntactial but must include the applicability of a whole array of grammatical and contextual
considerations. This condition has consequences separating

the two positions. First, common practice accepts only a certain number of nonexistent objects, those that have actually been introduced into stories, myths, jokes, make-believe situations, and the like. This is evidently a very large number, but it is not infinitely large as is the number of nonexistent objects admitted by Meinong. Second, common thought has a way of explaining just how nonexistent objects come to be: they are created in some act of composition or of the imagination. Meinong has no such explanation but must simply accept that there are nonexistent objects, leaving their origins unexplained. A third difference is that most of the odd examples in which Meinong so delighted are either not acceptable or if found acceptable have plausible explanations. Can there be contradictory objects? One simply tries to imagine stories containing them and lets the answer be determined by linguistic intuition. I have suggested that there might be round squares if stories including them are acceptable – as it seems to me they might. Yet surely one would be hard pressed to find acceptable stories including logically strange objects much more complex than this. Incomplete objects suffer a worse fate, since (as I argue in Chapter 6) fiction does not allow them when (as usual) it presupposes a background of logical completeness. The various cases Meinong offered can be judged by bringing them before the the bar of common practice; this provides both a decision procedure for their acceptability and also an explanation for why they turn out to be acceptable or not. The impression of the discovery of a new realm of entities, including some very peculiar logical species, does not attach to the position I have set out. Meinong is right, in the light of the analysis here, on the occurrence of genuine nonexistent objects and on their lack of existential standing. On the other hand, he can be faulted for not being sensitive to linguistic practice. Still, he called to our attention something that has generally been denied and devoted his life to understanding it, and for this the philosophical world is greatly in his debt.

4

FICTIONAL DISCOURSE

Issues centering around the nature and existential status of the fictional object are not the only ones to be dealt with in a full account of fictional language. Even if one is willing to grant that there are such items—that they are assumed in practice—one might wonder how reference and predication apply to them. In the case of public, physical objects, it is clear what it is for a thing to exist and to have properties. At least the phenomena to be accounted for are plain and overt, open to general examination, even if opinions might vary as to the right philosophical analysis of them. But nonexistent objects are not available in this way, and there may seem to be a deep mystery how there could ever come to be such things and how they could bear properties. The origins of familiar material entities and their property-sustaining features are clear enough, but how could items that have no existence whatever come to be, and to have properties? The answer, I suggest, is illuminated by considering the practice of telling a story. Noticing the conditions that make this activity acceptable clarifies the genesis of nonexistent objects and offers an opportunity to explain how they can have properties. Storytelling is just one of the uses of language in which references to fictions appear, and it is useful to distinguish it from two others; this helps clarify the role of the operator "in the story" and allows the solution of various philosophical puzzles arising for fiction. In this chapter I consolidate previous conclusions by examining the larger context in which fictional language occurs and by pointing out distinctions between the different types of statement constituitive of it. These reflections should round out the overall position I am presenting and help to weaken reservations about its philosophical plausibility.

Let me remark that I am concerned primarily with a specific kind of fiction—novels and stories having to do with normal human beings in realistic kinds of situation. Much of what is thought of as great literature falls into this category, familiar genres being epic and historical novels, tales of adventure and intrigue, stories of manners, romances, and detective fiction. Of less immediate concern are such forms as myth, fairy stories, fantasy, and science fiction, because these obey a somewhat different set of conventions and serve perhaps a different set of purposes. Modernist writing, for instance Pirandello's *Six Characters in Search of an Author*, suspends or manipulates the conventions I wish to point out. The reason for this focus is that realistic fiction is, I believe, philosophically fundamental. It is that genre which deals with real-life situations and so that which is used in expressing the deepest human concerns; it has certainly had a central place in Western literature. More important for our purposes, this genre is presupposed by at least some of these other modes; one who did not understand the conventions of realism would not be able to grasp the point of Pirandello's play, for Pirandello intends to mock these very conventions by self-consciously and pointedly violating them. Realism may not be presupposed in this way by all forms of imaginative thinking (possibly not by fairy stories or myth, for example); nevertheless, the logical principles in play in these other forms can be explained (mutatis mutandis) by a structure exhibited quite clearly in realistic writing. I do not argue explicitly for these claims, but I think that it is fairly clear how they might be filled out, and in Chapter 6 there are remarks on myth, dreams, and certain other forms of representation that provide support for them. In any case, realistic literature has been at the center of philosophical interest in fiction and is certainly rich enough to merit its own study.

THE ORIGINS OF NONEXISTENT OBJECTS: STORYTELLING

To deal with the perplexity about how there could ever be such things as simply nonexistent objects, let us return to the situation in which the conceptual apparatus generating them is adopted. What are the conditions for this? Imagine a society of human beings who speak a language much like English, but whose uses of language are entirely literal and concern only real objects. These speakers are accustomed to talking about familiar commonsense and other entities in their presence, and they accept remarks about existing nonpresent things and about future and past events. They have the concept of a nonexistent object, but only of a real nonexistent object. They acknowledge, for example, that dodos no longer exist although they did at one time, and they realize that in the future there will be people born who are not now in existence. Yet among these speakers there is no imaginative literature—no novels and stories, no telling of jokes except about things conceived in actual or possible historical situations, no myths, no bedtime or fairy stories, no tales of the supernatural. Their pictorial art is correspondingly limited—no plays or movies about (what we accept as) purely imaginary situations. We never find these people reporting their dreams, for the concept of an unreal dream figure is unknown to them; or, alternately, their dream reports are believed to be about existing things. Their religious beings are taken to be absolutely real and historical. In short, they do not have the concept of a fictional object: they have not adopted the rules pointed out in the previous chapter which allow references to merely conceptual objects; they do not play the language game of fictional discourse. Such a society is quite conceivable, I believe, although we might be inclined to think that these individuals are quite different from us and we would look for some explanation for the difference: is there a moral or religious prohibition against imaginative thought? is there some subtle physiological difference that accounts for the absence of dreaming or the enjoyment of stories? Whatever the explanation, this situation seems a possible one.

Now suppose that a mature, intelligent, well-respected member of this society, Zog, begins one day to speak to a group of listeners as follows: "Once upon a time in the distant past there was a crow ten times larger than any crow we have ever seen, and this crow lived at the top of the largest mountain. One day it flew down upon a town like ours and captured the fairest maiden living there in its claws and then took her back to its cave, and there it wanted to make her his wife." Zog goes on for some time in this vein. It is easy to imagine his audience following this performance, wondering what is going to happen next, becoming absorbed in the events recounted, hoping that things turn out well for the maiden and the crow. All of these are entirely natural reactions to such accounts, and so far they can be explained as responses by Zog's listeners to what they are taking to be a factual report of historical events. But suppose at the end of his performance Zog says, after it is clear that his audience has been understanding and enjoying his narration, "and none of this happened." How is his audience to react? One response would be to hold that Zog's words are meaningless, since they lack historical referents in violation of the accepted semantical practices of this tribe. This would, however, be extreme in view of the evident intelligibility of Zog's performance and the interest and pleasure generally taken in it. A second possible response would be to claim that, since Zog's sentences are so evidently understandable, there must be real referents somewhere, having subsistence or existing in some possible world (as tribal philosophers might suggest). Yet it might be noticed that Zog could have talked about things and situations that contained overt, or perhaps less controversially, hidden contradictions (a story about a round-square hoop, or about someone's squaring the circle), and this might make the assumption of real but merely possible referents less attractive. Or Zog might be thought of as simply lying, as telling an extended falsehood. But his listeners would realize that they enjoyed Zog's performance and did not feel themselves deceived, particularly as Zog had nothing to gain by his actions and did not seem to be attempting to trick or confuse the members of his audience. Rather, he seemed to be trying to entertain them.

In any case, there is a fourth reaction available: Zog's listeners simply begin talking among themselves about the events and figures in his narration without any assumption of existential status. When someone who has not been present at Zog's performance asks about the location of the town where the maiden lived and what family she belongs to, members of Zog's audience find it appropriate to say, "She did not exist at all and Zog simply made her up." Zog's hearers and his entire speech community could simply adopt linguistic practices corresponding to those I have outlined in the previous chapter. I am not suggesting that these four responses are the only ones possible (no doubt there are others), or that this last response is somehow better or more defensible philosophically than any of the alternatives. Questions of evaluation or justification are not at issue; rather, I am pointing out that this fourth response is a very natural one for humans beings to make when initially confronted with the possibility of storytelling.

My point is that this last reaction is quite intelligible to us as members of the same species as Zog and his community, for it is easy for us to imagine ourselves doing the same in those circumstances. And so doing does not involve any philosophical commitments other than those I have discussed in the previous chapter. The sheer acceptance of this new way of talking, according to which fictional characters and events are nonexistent tout court, is an option a speech community may well exercise because its members simply find stories absorbing, fun, instructive, profound, and revealing. It is just a native human capacity to understand stories and to enjoy them—with the implicit assumption that what are being talked about are objects having no ontological standing. We just do have the ability to produce and find intelligible the kinds of sentences and their included references which the above scenario illustrates—and no further explanation of this ability, in terms of the existential status of the objects and situations involved, is required. This is the basic answer to the question of how it is possible that there can be reference to nonexistent objects and the attribution of properties to them. Human beings in command of literal speech simply possess the capacity to begin speaking with the intention of telling a story (as we would put it), and their audiences are able to understand the story as so intended. Finding such speech intelligible and enjoyable, a linguistic community could take the further step of accepting it generally and thus incorporating the rules for its production and the concepts it includes into their overall conceptual scheme. It would then teach these rules and concepts to new members of the community. Children would be taught that certain bodies of discourse were not about anything real but about purely nonexistent objects. Nonnative speakers might have to add to their conceptual repertoire. The language game of fiction would then have become part of the conceptual scheme of this community.

There are several remarks to be made now in clarification. First, I am not suggesting that at some historical mo-

ment the language game of fictional discourse was introduced in this overt and self-conscious way through three
stages; these remarks are not historical conjectures and
this thought experiment is meant only to dramatize the
logically secondary status of the language of fiction. What
the conceivability of this imaginary situation shows is that
the various practices concerning fiction are logically dis-
pensible and have an optional status; they can be adopted
only when literal usage is already in place. This is the second point: the language of fiction is conceptually secondary
to literal speaking. Reference to real, familiar things and
verification of claims about them is fundamental to any
language, for without such a possibility one could not be
said to have mastered language of any sort. There would be
no way to establish that someone had really understood a
kind term as opposed to merely seeming to; literal discourse is basic to all language. There is a further type of
dependency, reflecting specifically fictional uses of language: one must be credited with mastery of the vocabulary of the everyday world before being said to understand
fiction, since fiction centrally employs this vocabulary for
its own characteristic purposes. Let me emphasize that
these considerations are conceptual, concerning what we
can conceive, and not empirical. It may be that as a matter
of actual fact one learns fictional language only after having learned literal speech. My contention has been a different one, that it is logically incoherent to try to conceive
the reverse order: describing someone as understanding stories without being able to apply the concepts employed in
them in real situations describes someone who has not satisfied our chief criterion for understanding those concepts,
and who therefore cannot be said to understand the sentences in which those concepts appear.

Adopting the practice of telling and understanding stories includes recounting the contents of a story to someone
else, commenting on parts of it and evaluating it, compar-

ing characters in one story with those in another and with
real people, and analyzing characters and fictional situations. One may refer to a character and predicate some
property of her from a standpoint outside the fiction—a usage I discuss shortly. Such remarks may be true or false. It
may seem puzzling that a statement about a character but
not entailed by the sentences constituting the contents of
the story can have a truth value, indeed can be true. It is
certainly true that Sherlock Holmes is more perceptive
than Watson, although this is not directly stated in the
Holmes stories. A nonexistent object having properties!—
and there is a pull in the direction of thinking that fictions
must have sort of real existence after all. Let me comment
on one aspect of this issue by anticipating a future discussion (Chapter 6). Works of fiction are written against a
background that fills in properties of the characters and situations. Part of this background for Conan Doyle's stories
is the assumption of normality, and by relying on this and
recalling the events of the stories we can infer that Holmes
was indeed the more perceptive. We can do this simply because the whole of the logical apparatus of factual discourse is taken over into fiction and discussions of fiction.
Not only are reference and predication in the telling of a
story licensed, but such practices as comparing the events
of this story with others and with real things or making
inferences from the contents of a fiction to the properties
of a character are as well. The considerations of the previous chapter denying the need for a separate realm of entities as underlying reference can be repeated here to establish a similar thesis for these practices. The implications
are similar: to say that a fictional object has a property is
simply to say that statements mentioning properties are accepted as being about such objects—statements having references to fictions in their subject positions can contain
expressions mentioning attributes in their predicate positions. The puzzle about how nonexistent objects can have

properties arises from an application of the model of predication about physical objects to the case of fiction; yet the
cases are relevantly different, the difference between reality
and fiction.

Finally, there might be a question about where Zog got
his storytelling practices. Did he acquire them from a storytelling culture? If he did, there is still the question of
how such a practice could get started in the first place. It is,
however, perfectly conceivable that Zog simply began to
speak in this way—or rather, that he realized that it was
possible to tell a story, and he simply told one. This possibility could have been suggested in various ways—some remark made by one of his children, or a sudden realization
during a tribal religious ceremony that the deities being
spoken of might not be real but—fictional! Zog is a completely competent speaker of his native language, so he is
in a position to use language in this new way. Previously
he lacked the concept of using language to tell a story and
so could not have had the intention to tell one. His great
realization was that it was possible to use common speech
for this new purpose of storytelling. Zog would have been a
genius in the situation I have pictured—which is artificial
enough, from a historical point of view. It is more realistic
to suppose that fictional and literal uses of language originated together; most probably there are no actual Zogs. But
the tale of Zog dramatizes important facts about fiction:
that it is conceptually parasitic on literal language, and
that it is a part of our conceptual equipment simply because it has been adopted as an intelligible and interesting
form of language.

The introduction of storytelling as an accepted practice
might in some respects be compared to the introduction of
the practice of playing games. Imagine a society in which
no one ever plays any game but in which all activities are
serious and are meant to satisfy physical desires and social
needs. One day someone puts pieces on a board and begins

moving them around, teaches others how to move them, and further explains that the point of all this is to try to bring about winning, a situation defined entirely in terms of board parameters. Such an individual would have made the same kind of innovation as Zog: an entirely new activity based on the introduction and acceptance of hitherto unknown conceptions would have been adopted in this culture. The question how it is possible that such phenomena as games (with their included moves and goals) could come to be is in many ways logically on a par with the question how such a thing as fictional discourse (with its nonexistent characters and events) could come to be. There are various types of answer to this question. It may be a neurophysiological fact that the human brain and nervous system are so constructed that we as a species have the capacity to grasp fictional uses of language. One can perhaps imagine a species of language-using creatures who for physiological reasons can use language literally but not for nonexistent objects. Or cognitive psychologists might attempt to discover the kinds of experience required for humans to learn fiction; possibly there are humans who learn literal usage but who never enter situations in which they learn fictional discourse. But my account of how it is possible is not intended as empirical. Instead, I mean to point out the conditions in which it is intelligible that people adopt fictional discourse, and here the comparison with adopting the practice of playing games is helpful. In both cases there is sheer conceptual innovation, or at least the elevation of the conception of an activity to the status of a public practice where that practice was not previously generally adopted in the society in question. The conditions in this sense for adopting game playing would be such matters as the occurrence in the culture of goal-directed activities, the possibility of mutual commitments to rule-governed actions, the enjoyments of competition, the acceptance of winning and losing within a context of amusement. For fiction, the conditions are such as have been pointed out above, the currency of literal uses of general terms and the practice of referring to real things by proper names and other forms of language. In a situation where these conditions are satisfied it becomes perfectly understandable that fictional discourse is introduced and accepted; if these conditions are not satisfied, its adoption is describable only in terms whose applicability is undermined by the failure of these conditions to be satisfied. In saying that humans simply have the ability to understand fictional language, I am pointing to a capacity of the human species which indeed we could have lacked. Even if the conditions for intelligibility are satisfied, it could have turned out that the creatures in question simply did not have the capacity to understand reference to nonexistent objects and predications of them. That we have this capacity may be physiologically explained by the possession of a highly evolved nervous system, and further it may be an empirical fact that specific experiences are required to learn such usage (as learning is required to play games). But the phenomenon I am pointing to is the capacity itself, no matter how explained physiologically or under what empirical conditions realized. Drawing attention to this capacity and to the conditions under which it is intelligible that it be exercised is pointing to the foundations of the language game of fiction; this brings out the interplay between linguistic practice and features of the world which make it clear in a distinctively philosophical way how there can be such practice.[1]

It might appear that there is a problem about the methodology I have been employing: the ability to tell a story is

---

1 The notion I am drawing on here is Wittgenstein's concept of "a very general fact of nature" and the idea of making it intelligible that a certain conceptual practice should apply given such general facts. See Ludwig Wittgenstein, *Philosophical Investigations*, 3rd ed. (New York: Macmillan, 1958), e.g., p. 230.

based on the prior capacity to think about imaginary figures and put them into a story and then to tell the story
out loud, someone might say. People can think up stories
in their head, and then they can tell them out loud if they
want to. So this is the basic capacity underlying talk about
nonexistent objects and not the public act of referring. In
one way this point does not raise an objection, for nothing
of importance as far as this account of fiction goes turns on
the thesis that the public activity of telling a story is the
foundation of fictional discourse. Rather, my claim is that
this activity exhibits the conceptual structure implicit in
thinking about the nonexistent and thus indicates (among
other things) what nonexistent objects are and how it is
that they can bear properties. Still, I do hold that it would
be a mistake to believe that there must always be some
temporally prior process of making up a story "in the
mind" which has the effect of producing physical sentences.
When one tells a story to an audience, there are not two
processes occurring, a private, purely mental one and in
consequence of this a public, physical one. This philosophical myth has been widely attacked and there is no reason
to rehearse the arguments against it.[2] I emphasize the possibility of a public adoption of a framework incorporating
the nonexistent because here the phenomena I wish to emphasize are overt and easily discerned. My imaginary case
could have concerned an individual who thought only
about real things and suddenly realized that he could think
about the nonexistent and began to tell himself stories
about it. His account of these new thoughts and the objects
they correspond to could be along the lines indicated
above: the objects are merely intentional and do not have
any existential status. There could indeed be such a case—
but then we need to know the grounds for attributing such

2 See Gibert Ryle, *The Concept of Mind* (New York: Barnes and Noble,
1949), e.g. chap. 2 ("In My Head," pp. 35–40).

objects to this individual, and these could only be the possibility of his making public references to them. So once
again we are returned from private, purely mental events to
a public situation. One might as well begin with public
language and derive conclusions directly from it. Perhaps it
needs to be said that this procedure of appealing to public
discourse implies no denial of distinctively mental occurrences of thinking about the nonexistent. There is no reason to deny that there are such events, on the contrary
there is very good reason to hold that they do occur. Nevertheless, the basic justification for supposing that they do
is the capacity of thinkers to tell stories and comment on
fictional situations. One might say that public speech depends on the capacity to think, but then thinking is not
logically independent of public speaking, and so this point
does not call into question the procedure I have employed;
when rightly understood, it supports it.

CONSTRUCTING, REPORTING, AND COMMENTING ON FICTION

The practice of storytelling Zog introduced into his tribe
will come to require various relatively distinct uses of language as stories become reported and discussed. Three such
uses are important to distinguish: those employed by a storyteller or author in setting out the contents of the tale,
those used in reporting those contents, and those expressing judgments about various elements in the story but
taking a standpoint external to it. I want now to describe
these uses. In the next section, I put this analysis to work
to solve certain perplexities arising with regard to fiction.

First, there are the remarks made in the very telling of
the tale. These present the imaginary situation with its
component characters and events. An author might write a
story about an individual whom she simply invents: she

has created, or made up, a character, as we say, in writing
sentences containing references to him and descriptions
about him. The events in her narrative are entirely made
up by her, or if her characters and plot have a historical
basis she is creating them in the sense that she is basing
them on history and not reporting the actual events—a
point to be considered at length in Chapter 6. These characters and events taken in their implied contextual situation constitute what I have been calling a fictional world;
the items in this world are merely conceptual, as I have
been putting it, and have no existential standing. The sentences the author uses have primarily a creative function
and do not report anything; it would not be expected that
they have truth values. If someone were to interrupt a storyteller with the remark, "No, what you just said was
false" or even "Yes, that is quite true," this would show a
misunderstanding of the language of storytelling. Storytellers' sentences are not used to make claims about independently existing states of affairs but to construct a fictional situation that can then become a subject matter for
commentary, so sentences appearing in the text of a novel
have no truth value and themselves serve as criteria for the
truth-values of assertions about the contents of the novel.[3]
Realistic fiction does of course include broad and indefinite
requirements of consistency and plausibility. Conan Doyle
cannot have Holmes suddenly short and fat or riding to his
next case on Pegasus or meeting Watson for lunch on the
moon—for he is writing within the constraints of a certain

---

3 This claim holds even for sentences about abstractions, e.g., "There is
no greatest prime number." This might appear to be true *ueberhaupt* and
so to transcend the limits of its story. However, appearing in the text of a
fiction it does not make a general claim but merely establishes the mathematical facts for the world of the story. We can imagine a tale including
the negation of this sentence. In that story there would be a greatest
prime; clearly no claim to general truth is being made here. It is plausibility within genre that sets the limits on acceptable sentences of this
kind and not "real" truth (see Chapter 6).

literary genre, the detective story. Yet within these constraints he can give Holmes any properties he finds suitable—a topic I investigate in Chapter 6.

What about the names and definite descriptions in the
text of a story; if they have a constructive function, can
they include references, as I have been holding? It has been
claimed, by J. O. Urmson, among others, that authors do
not refer in the course of composing a story: "What I am
saying is that making up a fiction is not a case of stating, or
asserting, or propounding a proposition and includes no
acts such as referring."[4] In the previous chapters I have already discussed the issue of reference to fictions, but perhaps Urmson's claim can be construed as being restricted
to sentences constructing fiction and contending that in
these cases there is no reference, regardless of what happens in other uses of language about fictions. This claim
may be based on an a priori view of reference which limits
it to real things, and on this view the claim is true. But
such views have their problems, as we see in Chapter 2. If
instead reference in stories is being denied solely on the
ground that sentences in fictions make up the imaginary
situation and do not report anything, then (quite apart from
earlier considerations) the inference is not in general plausible. There may be some initial appeal to denying reference
for names and the like used to *introduce* a character into a
story (as in a story that begins "Albert Swenson was accustomed to look out over the mountains every morning as he
walked to his barn to milk his cows"), for a reader need not
have prior knowledge of any real or fictional person named
Albert Swenson to understand this sentence. So how could
there be genuine reference, even in the speech act sense
elaborated in the previous chapter? Still, the phenomena
characteristic of reference can be perceived here: a reader

4 J. O. Urmson, "Fiction," *American Philosophical Quarterly* 13
(1976): 155.

knows that this is the first sentence in a novel—a literary
form typically including characters—and so naturally takes
this sentence to be presenting one of them. Here the author's act of referring does not presuppose some independently occurring figure to whom a reader's attention is to
be drawn; rather, the very act of referring in this special
context both introduces the object and calls the reader's
attention to it. The use of a referring expression can have
this double function only in such a context as this. And
there is even less reluctance to admit reference later on in
the story, when the fictional world is well constructed. For
example, when at the end of a tale one comes to "As I
turned away I saw Holmes, with his back against a rock
and his arms folded, gazing down at the rush of the wa-
ters,"[5] then only someone with extreme theoretical commitments could deny reference for the name and pronouns.
   Whatever view one comes to here, it is clear that this
creative use of language results in something about which
references and assertions can be made by commentators
and critics. A story or novel has *contents*. Once written
out, the contents of a narrative can be reported, made the
subject of claims that can be true or false, investigated in
various ways, compared with other such contents, and the
like. Such usages constitute the second kind of activity to
which I am calling attention. The contents of a story—its
fictional world—have an independent status that can be
learned by anyone who reads it. These contents are objective and independent of individual belief in this way:
whether a certain character is in a story or whether a given
state of affairs holds there are not matters of arbitrary belief; rather, these depend on what the sentences setting out
the story say. Remarks purporting to report contents have

5 A. Conan Doyle, "The Adventure of the Final Problem," in *The Original Illustrated Sherlock Holmes* (Secaucus, N.J.: Castle Books, 1979), p.
338.

truth values. There is full warrant for marking (1) true on an examination and (2) false;

(1) Sherlock Holmes smokes a pipe
(2) Sherlock Holmes plays the flute

And although the following is never overtly stated in the narrative, it is obviously true:

(3) Holmes is more perceptive than Watson

To statements intended to report the contents of a fiction we can prefix "in the story/novel/myth . . ." or "the story says that . . ."; I call any such statement an "inside" statement. To decide whether an inside statement is true one must consult the contents of the relevant text, done typically by the prosaic(!) procedure of reading it and simply noticing whether the situation described or implied in the story is as the statement asserts. The truth conditions of such assertions are the "sayso" of the fiction, as it has been aptly put.[6] I am not here concerned with the question of what exactly *is* the content of a story; this controversial matter is considered in Chapter 6. Here I am only pointing out that there is such a thing and indicating something about the kinds of sentence used in constructing and reporting it.

There is a third category of uses of sentences concerning fiction which stands in contrast to both the previous two. This category is illustrated by

(4) Holmes is my favorite fictional detective

and

6 The term originates with John Woods; see, e.g., *The Logic of Fiction: A Philosophical Sounding of Deviant Logic* (The Hague: Mouton, 1974).

(5) Holmes was created by Arthur Conan Doyle

Such remarks cannot be prefixed by "in the story," and their truth conditions are not the contents of the story but empirical reality. They are typically made by a reader commenting on something that appears in the fiction and claiming that it has some property external to the fictional world; I call these "outside" assertions. Here it is even more difficult to deny reference to fictional items; even those who reject it for sentences consituting the text of a literary work grant it for this case.[7]

There are then three kinds of locution to be kept separate: those appearing in the narrative itself and functioning to construct the fictional situation, those purporting to report the contents of a situation so set out, and those about some item in a fiction but attributing to it some property external to the work itself. There are perhaps other sentences about fiction not falling neatly into one of the above categories; for example,

(6) Sherlock Holmes is taller than Hercule Poirot

This example seems best placed in the second class, since its truth conditions are not external reality but the contents of literary works. There is no one story that contains both Holmes and Poirot, and so there is no operator that can be prefixed to (6). Perhaps what we do in ascertaining the truth value is imagine a single fictional world in which both detectives appear and where their heights can be compared. Whatever the right analysis of (6), the classifications introduced here are firm enough for present purposes.

The considerations above can be utilized to clarify fur-

---

7 See Urmson, "Fiction," p. 155; Searle's admission of reference here was mentioned in Chapter 2.

ther the notion of a fictional object. It is part of the contentu of Conan Doyle's stories that Sherlock Holmes smokes a pipe; certainly in stories fictional characters have empirical predicates. It is also true that Holmes was created by Conan Doyle; it was he who wrote the Holmes stories and not anyone else. So one and the same thing can have the properties of being a pipe smoker and being created by Conan Doyle. Now how can all this be, one might wonder, since these properties belong to different logical categories. Pipe smokers are creatures existing in time and space and having certain bodily organs; yet what is created by Conan Doyle (in the relevant sense) is not anything existing in time and space but a fiction, a nonexistent object. In any case, it might seem perplexing that a nonexistent object could have empirical properties.[8] This consideration brings into clear focus the notion of an object I am employing. In the case of a real object, something existing independently of language or thought about it, the thing has its properties in its own right and regardless of what anyone might think they are. It is this independent existence that makes it available for reference. Descriptions of it or theories about it are intended to represent the independent states of affairs in which it participates. Ordinary examinations or scientific investigations are the means whereby these properties are discovered, the supposition being that there are ways of finding out just what these properties are. Objects of such investigations are conceived to fall into different conceptual types (assuming that there are different types of object), where each type of thing has its distinctive set of attributes. Spatiotemporal entities have one set of properties, abstractions another, and so on through however many types one admits. For real things, then, features characteristic of different conceptual types cannot belong

8 Van Inwagen raises this question; I consider his specific way of dealing with it in Chapter 5.

to the same entity. And on this model of an object, it would be impossible to have such disparate features as "smoking a pipe" and "being created by Conan Doyle" holding of the same thing. My thesis throughout has been that there is a different notion of an object accepted in common thought, that of a mere referent or grammatical object. An object on this notion is *just* what corresponds to accepted linguistic practice and is nothing metaphysically over and above it; it is not independent of language or thought and is an object only in the sense that references and predications (and truth-valued claims and the like) are accepted about it. It is made available for reference only through thought or language itself and not through having prior, independent status. Such objects belong to the conceptual category of the unreal and have properties just in that property-attributing expressions are appropriately applied to them in types of discourse such as fiction and myth. Whether these expressions are truly or falsely applied depends on purely linguistic or conceptual considerations and not on external, independent reality. Given this analysis, it is not surprising that fictional characters have both empirical properties and ones typically belonging to abstractions. That Holmes smokes a pipe and was created by Conan Doyle means merely that there are contexts in which Holmes can be truly said to smoke a pipe and other contexts in which he can be truly said to have been created by Conan Doyle. These two kinds of context are not logically alike. Predications of the former, empirical type can be truly made only in inside statements—ones governed by the "in the story" operator. Those of the later, conceptual variety are true only if appearing in outside statements (to use my terminology). The concept of a fictional character is such that it allows predications in both sorts of context. Yet while it is true that Holmes both smokes a pipe and was created by Conan Doyle, it would be misleading straightforwardly to assert this, for this could be taken to imply that both predications have the same truth conditions; at any rate, such an assertion fails to indicate that different contexts hold. The facts are less confusingly expressed in some such way as this: Conan Doyle wrote a series of stories about Sherlock Holmes, who is said in them to smoke a pipe. Such an assertion gives the predicates their appropriate contexts. The empirical property is attributed only in an inside context and the abstract one only in an outside context, and there is no suggestion of the properties being on a conceptual par. In any case, once it is realized that fictions are objects only in the sense of being acceptable referents and not in the sense of having independent existential status, any reluctance to grant the attribution of both empirical and abstract qualities to the same object should disappear.[9]

TWO PUZZLING CASES

Toward the end of "On Denoting," Russell wrote:

A logical theory may be tested by its capacity for dealing with puzzles, and it is a wholesome plan, in thinking about logic, to

---

9 Fictions are not the only conceptual objects commonly accepted; there are, e.g., direct objects (see Chapter 3). This issue is discussed further in later chapters. I remark now that it seems plausible to explain the introduction of abstractions such as goodness, redness, and even numbers more or less along the lines given for literary fictions. The introduction of abstractions or universals as grammatical objects would occur through the process of nominalizing adjectives: it is natural to go from "x is good" to "the goodness of x." There is a similar movement possible for numbers: from "there is a pair of cows there" to "the cows there number two" to "two is the number of cows there," or some such progression. But these issues have their own complexities and I certainly do not wish to suggest that conclusions about fictions can be straightforwardly transferred to them. Nevertheless, this analysis of fiction is certainly suggestive for the analysis of nonconcrete objects generally—naturally a large, further project.

stock the mind with as many puzzles as possible, since these
serve much the same purpose as is served by experiments in
physical science.[10]

His point was that a theory ought to be able to deal with
conceptual data that are initially perplexing, and there is
plenty of that with regard to nonbeing. I have been sorting
out conceptual issues all along—the status of the nonexistent, as a primary example—and I do more of this in the
chapters to follow. Here I want to look at certain prima facie
difficulties—Russell would call them puzzles—and show
that foregoing considerations handle them nicely.

First consider

(7) Sherlock Holmes does not exist

This statement is true if taken as an outside statement.
And yet the corresponding inside statement,

(7a) In the story, Holmes does not exist

is false. In the tale, Holmes does exist; he is real there and
not a fiction within a fiction (as would be a character in a
story Holmes read). Suppose (achronologically) that in one
of Conan Doyle's pieces Holmes reads a Hercule Poirot
mystery; then there might be

(8) In the story, Holmes read in a story that Hercule Poirot was
short

Poirot exists in the story within the story but not in the
primary story, the one about Holmes. Fictions (storytelling,
myths, dreams, etc.) can be embedded within fiction; con-

10 Bertrand Russell, "On Denoting," in *Logic and Knowledge*, ed. Robert C. Marsh (London: George Allen and Unwin, 1956), p. 47.

sequently, existence claims are relevant to context — to the relevant rule or to reality if no fiction operator applies. Nevertheless, this is also true:

(9) Sherlock Holmes is a fictional character

This is of course an outside remark; it has a different truth-value from

(9a) In the story, Sherlock Holmes is a fictional character

which is false for the relevant works. It is, however, part of the concept of a fictional character that characters do not exist, and since Holmes is one of these [i.e., (9) is true], (7) follows. There is also the (outside) fact asserted by

(5) Holmes was created by Arthur Conan Doyle

This statement taken with (7) gives the astounding result that Conan Doyle created something that does not exist. This sounds very strange: Holmes does not exist but nevertheless was created, and furthermore he exists in stories. There might even be the situation of a narrative in which Holmes does not exist but in a fiction in that fiction he does—and so on through countless variations on these themes. This is all only philosophical bafflement; matters are kept straight by remembering the context or truth conditions of each of these assertions. That historically Holmes did not exist is quite consistent with the fact that he is a character in a story; that he was created simply means that an author used certain expressions under the rubric of certain conventions.

This untangling seems straightforward enough. There is, however, a more perplexing conflict and one whose solution is I think quite illuminating. Consider the outside truth

(10) There is (actually exists) a fictional character, Sherlock Holmes

It is a fact that Arthur Conan Doyle wrote a series of stories having a detective, Sherlock Holmes, as their main character. This is a fact about the literature of the late nineteenth century, as anyone can discover by making the appropriate investigations. On the other hand,

(7) Sherlock Holmes does not exist

is undeniable; Holmes is a fictional character and ipso facto nonexistent. Surely (10) and (7) are about the same object, the well-known nineteenth-century literary creation. The consequence seems to be that the same thing both exists (through being a recognized fictional character) and does not exist (in virtue of this very fact). This is especially perplexing because it cannot be resolved by appealing to different contexts, as in the solution of the previous case. Both (10) and (7) are outside truths and indeed appeal to the same set of facts as truth conditions. Nevertheless, this second puzzle can be dealt with by noticing that although (10) and (7) are about the same object they make very different types of claim about it. The remark that there is a certain fictional character [e.g., (10)] implies that a set of names and descriptions ("Holmes," "the occupant of 221B Baker Street") appears in the text of a story that is to be read with the understanding that its author intends these expressions to introduce and be about a figure in this story. They are about this character merely in the sense of making appropriate the employment of these and other expressions in further referring uses in inside and outside assertions. To say that there is a certain fictional character is to claim that there is a set of sentences used in writing a work of fiction and containing certain referring expressions, where the understanding is that such sentences

make appropriate the referring use of these and related expressions in further, inside and outside, sentences. Yet to
say that there is a certain character is to imply that nothing
really existing corresponds to these referring uses; what is
given in the introduction of a character is merely a grammatical object, to use my terminology. One can state the
facts by alluding solely to uses of language, or one can employ the apparently more ontological idiom of "kinds of object"—as Anscombe noted with regard to direct objects (see
Chapter 3, n. 9). In either case, nothing external to the body
of fictional writing in question is implied. All this recapitu-
lates the discussion of the previous chapter, but in terms of
the three kinds of assertion distinguished in the previous
section.

It is important to see that these two statements while
about the same object assume very different perspectives
on it and make different types of claim about it. Statement
(10) is a contingent truth asserting the appearance of a particular fictional character in a given body of writings and
thereby implying the occurrence of certain expressions in a
text to be understood as imaginative and not historical.
These writings need not have appeared: Conan Doyle
might have chosen to write about a military officer not
named Sherlock Holmes who did not solve crimes, or he
might not have written fiction at all. Statement (7) makes a
different kind of claim: that the references Conan Doyle's
writing include and make appropriate are not to anything
real. Clearly (7) does not deny what (10) asserts, the occurrence of "Holmes" and other expressions in the text of a
work of fiction. On the contrary (7) assumes them since if
there were no character Holmes—no writing of the appropriate sort—(7) could not be true since then "Holmes"
would not have the kind of reference (7) requires. This
therefore is the essential consideration: (7) contains a reference to the very object introduced by the uses of language
implied to occur by (10). The grammatical object estab-

lished by the facts alluded to in (10) is what is referred to in (7); (10) is both a condition for (7) and also entails it.

It is a consequence of this fact that (7) is not contingent: it does not just happen that Holmes does not exist. The conceptual category to which a fictional character belongs is that of something available for reference only, a mere referent and not something that could exist. This claim can be given further support by considering how (7) is to be appropriately expanded. Generally speaking, in a case of the denial of existence some further explanation can be provided indicating the way in which the item does not exist—the thing has become extinct, it has not yet been constructed, and so on. The proper expansion of (7) shows the conceptual type to which its object belongs. Here are some inappropriate expansions:

(7b) Sherlock Holmes did not exist in the late nineteenth century; he had died and was no longer alive then
(7c) Sherlock Holmes did not exist in the late nineteenth century; he had not been born yet

These are inappropriate because they imply that Sherlock Holmes is a real person who merely happened not to live in the late nineteenth century. Less obviously wrong is

(7d) Sherlock Holmes did not exist; he might have existed in history but he happened not to

I have already argued that (7d) cannot be the correct interpretation of the negative existential, for even if it were to be discovered that there had been a real person living in London at the appropriate time and bearing Holmes's characteristics, this would not have been Holmes the fictional character. The unreal and the contingently nonexistent are distinct logical categories. This character was created by

Arthur Conan Doyle by writing certain sentences, and no
ical person can be so created. Conan Doyle's writing falls
unquestionably into the genre of fiction (not history), and
so the individuals it concerns belong to the conceptual category of created literary fictions, to the unreal, and not to
that of the real but contingently nonexistent. So the plausible looking (7d) is not right either.

What (7) refers to is a grammatical object, and so the
proper expansion of (7) is

(7e) Sherlock Holmes did not exist; he is (belongs to the category of) a fictional character

This statement locates Holmes in his proper logical type:
fictitious entities necessarily do not exist and are merely
grammatical. Statement (7) then is noncontingently true.
Given the type of object Holmes is, he could not exist, and
(7)—or more perspicuously its expanded version (7c)—is a
conceptual truth that states this unambiguously. Notice
that these considerations do not assume any particular concept of existence, since (7e) denies Holmes's existence in
any sense. Statements (10) and (7) are related in this way,
then: (10) asserts the occurrence of a fictional character and
(7) states a necessary truth about this same character. One
is a contingent claim about the appearance of certain locutions in a literary work; the other makes the noncon-
tingent claim that the references licensed by these locutions are to a merely conceptual and so necessarily
nonexistent object.

This conceptual arrangement is not unique and is comparable to ones involving explicitly abstract objects; consider

(11) There is the hypothetical construct of the average American

and

(12) The average American does not exist

According to (11), a certain hypothetical construct has been introduced; it might not have been proposed but it happens to have been (let us grant). Statement (12) points out that the object mentioned in (11) does not exist. But (12) is a logical truth, as is made clear by its expansion

(12a) The average American does not exist; it is a hypothetical construct

The average American, qua hypothetical construct, could not exist; on the other hand, a real person having all the characteristics attributed to the average American would not be the average American of statistical theory but a real individual who just happened to have the right properties. You can talk to your neighbor and watch her put out her recycled newspapers; you cannot talk to an abstract object even if the abstraction is rightly said to have some of the characteristics your neighbor possesses. Again (11) is a species of empirical truth and (12) a conceptual one; they are far from incompatible but in some broad sense mutually entailing.

These two cases illustrate the capacity of the position I have set out to deal with the puzzling conceptual facts that arise in connection with fiction: the inside/outside distinction, the notion of a fictional world created in accordance with the rules of the language game of fiction, and other principles of everyday thought provide powerful tools for cutting through the conceptual thickets ("Meinong's jungle"?) springing up in the land of nonbeing. I would hope that a fair-minded schoolmaster, to change the figure, would think that the views I have advanced would pass Russell's test with high marks.

5

ALTERNATIVE REFERENTIAL
THEORIES OF FICTION

Recent times have seen a profusion of theories of fiction, many of which display marked sympathies with Meinong's view that there is genuine reference to objects commonly considered nonexistent. I examine two of these, those of van Inwagen and Parsons, and for very different reasons. Van Inwagen is attempting to give an account of the common notion of a fictional character, and many of the details of his analysis agree with those presented in this study. Still, his explanation of just what a fiction is differs sharply from my own, and it is important to make these differences clear. Parsons is interesting for a very different reason—for the basic methodological stance he uses to support acceptance of the nonexistent. Considering his position at some length gives me the opportunity to review various methodological issues and to defend my own procedures. In particular, it invites discussing whether, regardless of the commitments of common discourse, there really are non-existent objects.

VAN INWAGEN: FICTIONS
AS THEORETICAL ENTITIES

For van Inwagen a fictional character is a "creature of fiction," a kind of "theoretical entity of literary criticism."[1] Such fictional characters possess attributes such as being a character in a certain novel, having been created by an author, (perhaps) being a satiric figure. Strictly speaking, they do not have properties such as weighing 170 pounds, having a beaked nose, solving crimes. Sentences that apparently predicate these properties of fictions in fact only "ascribe" them, where ascription is a primitive, unanalyzable relation analogous to that which on Descartes's view is asserted in sentences such as "Jones is six feet tall." For Descartes, Jones is a mind and does not have physical properties; nevertheless, the Cartesian can allow this kind of sentence as a matter of practical convenience. Similarly, Sherlock Holmes is a theoretical entity and as such cannot have weight or perform actions even though ordinary sentences such as

(1) Sherlock Holmes smokes a pipe

express true propositions about him—propositions that must be analyzed in terms of the primitive notion of ascription.

This outlook has the advantage of recognizing that paraphrase and pretense theories of fictional sentences are inadequate and of acknowledging genuine reference to fictional characters without positing an extra realm of being. Nevertheless, it oversimplifies the conceptual situation in which references to fictions takes place; in particular, its

---

1 Peter van Inwagen, "Creatures of Fiction," *American Philosophical Quarterly* 4 (1977):299–308.

model of posits in the physical sciences leads to distortions
of the logical regularities concerning fictions Van Inwagen
thinks that when we say such things as (1) we cannot be
speaking literally, because this would be analyzing (1) as
the attribution of the empirical predicate "smokes a pipe"
to an abstract object, which is an absurdity. The conceptual
situation cannot, however, be analyzed in this straightforward way. A statement like (1) is an inside one and hence
tacitly carries "in the story"; the attribution of the empirical predicate occurs under the scope of the operator and
there the attribution is to an empirical object, not to an
abstract one. To put it more exactly, the language game of
fiction allows for contexts—inside contexts, in my terminology—where it is perfectly appropriate to couple the
name of a fictional character with a term standing for an
empirical property. At the same time, such couplings are
not allowed outside such contexts; the situation van Inwagen fears, the categorical and unqualified predication of
a physical property to an abstraction, is excluded by the
rules of fictional discourse. Indeed, this point is developed
more fully in Chapter 4.

Van Inwagen might reply by asking why this view of the
conceptual situation does not take a fictional character as a
physical object and not a nonconcrete one; he is evidently
concerned with what appear to be empirical attributions to
what we both acknowledge to be nonempirical objects. Van
Inwagen and I share the goal of making clear the conceptual status of a fictional object. His idea is that fictional
characters are logically just like theoretical entities (electrons, for example) in the physical sciences—things assumed in order to facilitate explanations of data.[2] This suggestion has the merits I have already mentioned. But it has
the considerable defect of not being able to provide for the
fact that the language game of fiction is conceptually much

2 Ibid., p. 303.

more complicated than that of particle physics—at least with regard to the issues relevant here. The reply I have offered above on van Inwagen's behalf, that fictions have become empirical objects if apparently unqualified empirical predications of them are allowed, disregards the fact that these predications are being admitted only in a context actually qualified by the fictional operator—an inside context. Thus when one raises the issue of the status of fictional characters generally within our conceptual scheme —the question of what kind of object in the absolute sense they are—the answer is what I have given earlier: a fictional character is a mere referent, to be denoted but not considered to have existential standing. So as far as their absolute classification is concerned, fictions are not empirical despite the occurrence of contexts in which empirical properties are allowed to be predicated of them. Van Inwagen is attempting to analyze the notion of a fictional character by taking as a model the concept of a theoretical entity in the physical sciences; this approach is not sensitive to the complexities holding for fiction. It has no place for the notion of a logical operator and the consequent distinction between inside and outside contexts, and it is this operator that makes possible the application of empirical predicates to fictions without the consequence that fictions must be finally classified as empirical objects.

Since on his conception fictional characters are abstract objects, van Inwagen must explain the currency of sentences apparently giving them empirical properties; he must explain how abstractions seem to bear empirical predicates. As we have seen, he undertakes this through the notion of "attribution," an unanalyzable primitive relation that takes at its model a Cartesian analysis of ascriptions of physical properties to a person. On Cartesian theory these ascriptions make the category mistake of attributing an empirical property to a nonphysical mind. In the van Inwagen is happy to discover a precedent for allow-

ing predications that are not strictly acceptable according
to theory. This comparison makes it clear, however, that
his account imputes an incoherence to ordinary fictional
discourse; from the perspective of a correct philosophical
analysis we are committing a category mistake in making
remarks such as "Holmes smokes a pipe," since abstract
objects cannot literally smoke pipes. This result itself
ought to make us uneasy with his analysis. He began attempting to present the notions embedded in a form of discourse that is perfectly understandable to everyone and
used universally without hesitation, and yet his account
implies that these uses of language are strictly incoherent.
This makes one feel that van Inwagen has not really gotten
at ordinary thinking about fiction. One would have expected an analysis showing how such a generally intelligible and unproblematic form of discourse is conceptually
possible, rather than one that ascribes a conceptual absurdity to it. Such misgivings parallel ones we have with Descartes's theory of mind–body relations: a theory that attributes an incoherence to a large part of the data on which the
theory is based thereby casts doubt on itself. Certainly according to the analysis elaborated in this study there is no
such incoherence in everyday fictional discourse; according
to it such sentences as (1) appear under the fictional operator where they are in order and require no double-think on
the part of readers. The model of assuming theoretical particles in the physical sciences has left no room for the du-
ality of contexts of fictional discourse which is crucial for
explaining actual usage here.

The physical posit model has misled van Inwagen in a
further way, into supposing that objects posited must exist.
If fictions are like electrons (or any physical posit), and
electrons exist, then fictional characters exist after all despite the fact that common discourse has them not existing. Thus van Inwagen must confront the ordinary acceptance of negative existentials. He has only one brief

comment on them: the situation with such assertions is "very complicated"; in making such a remark as "Mr. Pickwick does not exist," a speaker "would probably be expressing the proposition that there is no such man as Pickwick, or more precisely, the proposition that nothing *has* all the properties *ascribed to* Pickwick."[3] I have already discussed such a suggestion (see Chapter 3); this is not what such a speaker would mean, since even if there were a real man with all Pickwick's properties this would not falsify the denial. Imposition of the physical science model has again led van Inwagen astray.

Van Inwagen's theory has in common with ordinary practice the admission of fictions as genuine referents not inhabiting a world of subsistence. Yet he holds that they exist, not that they do not exist (much less that they belong to the category of the unreal); thus his views conflict with common belief, a conflict he cannot explain away. Further, he omits the distinction between inside and outside contexts—an omission that leads to an overly simple account of sentences containing empirical predications of fictional characters, itself implying incoherence in common linguistic practice. The comparison of fictions with theoretical entities is useful to the degree it allows one to grant fictions full objective status but is ultimately inadequate in that it leads to distortions in other areas.[4]

---

3 Ibid., p. 308, n. 11.

4 Nicholas Wolterstorff also proposes a non-paraphrase, non-pretense account of everyday names used for fictional characters. He holds that what we then refer to is a kind of person, a universal. What is referred to by "Chichikov" in Gogol's *Dead Souls* is the kind such that any instance of it must be a Russian, a confidence trickster, named Chichikov, etc.; *Works and Worlds of Art* (New York: Oxford University Press, 1980), pp. 144, 158–159. One objection to this theory, as to van Inwagen's, is that it conflicts with the common view that fictional characters do not exist— for universals of the sort Wolterstorff is suggesting do exist. Other decisive criticisms are given by Kendall L. Walton, "Review of *Works and Worlds of Art*," *Journal of Philosophy* 80 (1983):187–189.

PARSONS'S QUINEAN MEINONGIANISM
AND THE METHODOLOGY OF
NONEXISTENCE

As I noted in Chapter 1, Parsons has attempted to justify
the inclusion of nonexistent objects within the philosophical tradition established by Russell and represented in recent years by Quine. My interest in Parsons is not especially in the technical proposals he has made in the course
of setting out the details of his theory. These have been
commented on elsewhere and are advanced more in the
service of the formal semantics he develops than to capture
everyday conceptions.[5] Parsons's work is interesting here
because of his way of arguing for it. My concern in this
study is not only to put forward a view of the nonexistent
but also to support a way of doing philosophy—analysis of
the conceptual structures present in common thought—
through showing how it can deal successfully with the
problem of nonbeing. Parsons has an entirely different
methodology which he is careful to articulate, and I want
to argue that this does not fit well with his Meinongian
outlook. The broader issue here is the methodological
stance appropriate to a position admitting nonexistent objects; I take this opportunity to consider various ap-
proaches in the light of this question. Methodological issues may not be to everyone's taste, but they are
fundamental in philosophy and I believe that the topic of
nonbeing offers a particularly good test case for judging
them. If theories admitting nonexistent objects—the only
plausible view, given considerations that Meinongians
such as Parsons and myself both accept—cannot be conceived in terms of scientific theorizing, the appropriate alternative seems to be some sort of descriptive analysis.

5 See Robert Howell, *Journal of Philosophy* 80 (1983):163–173, and
William J. Rapaport, *NOUS* 19 (1985):255-271, for criticism and further
bibliography.

Parsons sees that there are many ordinary cases of apparent reference to nonexistent objects. These instances even pass one of the standard tests for reference, existential generalization, so appearances are born out.[6] Parsons then argues that attempts to provide paraphrases of the relevant sentences, heretofore the standard response in the orthodox tradition, do not work, or at least there is no compelling reason to resort to paraphrase. So "viewed impartially, [he believes] that there is nothing within the orthodox tradition to undercut the prima facie plausibility . . . that there are nonexistent objects."[7] So far, then, Parsons agrees with the conclusions I have put forward earlier. In his view, however, the considerations he has advanced establish prima facie plausibility only and not that there really are nonexistent objects, and Parsons is sensitive to the issue of how to go on from here or indeed whether one can go on without begging the question. In *Nonexistent Objects*, his view is that arriving at the above conclusion provides sufficient motivation for developing a theory of nonexistent objects "with the reasonable hope that it will turn out to be true." And "whether it *is* true or not will ultimately be decided in terms of global considerations—how well it accords with the data and with other theories, and how widespread and interesting its applications are. Only years of use and critical examination can answer such questions."[8]

Parsons's remarks in *Nonexistent Objects* leave it unclear just what kinds of "data" he has in mind here and what possible "applications" are of the hypothesis that there are nonexistent objects; answers are provided in "Are There Nonexistent Objects?" Here he accepts Quine's idea that "it is legitimate to assume that there are physical ob-

6 This test is given prominence in Terence Parsons, "Are There Nonexistent Objects?" *American Philosophical Quarterly* 19 (1982):365–371, and is perhaps implicit in the earlier discussion in *Nonexistent Objects* (New Haven, Conn.: Yale University Press, 1980), pp. 35–37.

7 Parsons, *Nonexistent Objects*, p. 37.

8 Ibid., p. 38.

jects because, among other things, this shared assumption
greatly simplifies reports of our experiences." He continues, "I claim that it is legitimate to assume that there
are nonexistent objects for exactly the same reason—it
simplifies reports of our experiences in exactly the same
way." His only illustration is that of a dream report, where
"the shared assumption that there is something I have been
dreaming about tells you as much about my dream experiences as the assumption that there are physical objects
does when I report my waking experiences."⁹ For Parsons,
dream entities, a species of nonexistent object, are as well
established as public objects and have exactly the same justification. Again he has applied orthodox Quinean procedures in coming to quite un-Quinean conclusions.

   Parsons's proposals represent an important development
in philosophical thought about nonexistence, both for the
claims made about nonexistent objects and for the applications of "orthodox" methodology supporting them. As indicated, I am interested in the methodology. One first wants
to know just how the Quinean standard of simplifying reports of experience applies to fictional characters or to typical Meinongian cases (the golden mountain, the round
square). On the face of it, we never (or do not normally)
have experiences that we find it natural to report by making references to such things. We refer to fictional characters on the basis of reading or hearing sentences produced
under the rubric of certain conventions. Normally such experiences do not produce images whose contents are naturally designated by the kinds of referring expression typically appearing in fiction. In dreams there are such images:
one speaks about Aunt Emily who appeared in a dream because one has had a dream image of Aunt Emily. This is far
from typical of understanding fiction, where normally one
just reads or hears a story and grasps its contents without

9 Parsons, "Are There Nonexistent Objects?" p. 370.

the occurrence of vivid imagery. Subsequent references to fictional characters are based on this grasp rather than on any imagery having distinctive pictorial content. This seems even more evident for the Meinongian examples: to understand "the golden mountain" one does not have to visualize a mountain, and in the case of "the round square" the possibility of an authentic image is doubtful indeed. The only experiences universally present to readers of stories are those of reading sentences in books—but these are quite unlike the dream imagery Parsons mentions, and the suggestion that one can make sense of perceptions of printed letters through using names and descriptions like "Sherlock Holmes" and "Watson's revolver" has no plausibility. The comparison of figures in dreams with physical objects has at least the rationale that in each case there is some perceptual experience that talk of objects can be supposed (on Quinean theory anyway) to explain; analogous perceptions are not found in the experience of reading or hearing sentences. Possibly Parsons has some other kind of experience in mind, yet none readily suggests itself, and it is just not clear what this could be if, on the crucial matter of simplifying experience, it must be comparable to dreaming. Perhaps Parsons can argue that at least the realm of dream objects constitutes a class of nonexistent objects to which his methodology applies. But if fictions and the familiar Meinongian cases lie outside the scope of his proposals, then these become vastly less interesting and his claim to have provided an account with the range of Meinongian theory is seriously undermined.

The problem here is Parsons's general conception of his project. It is clear that he regards it along the lines of a scientific investigation: there is good reason to think that there are entities of a certain type, so let theories explaining them be proposed with the most plausible among them to emerge on the application of standard criteria for theory construction. The entities in question differ from the usual empirical ones in being nonexistent; still, Parsons supposes that he has reasonable grounds for hypothesizing that there might be such things: there are "a host of particular propo- sitions which we believe and which seem to commit us to unreal objects" and which cannot be shown not to by the usual techniques.[10] Parsons's formal proposals developed in *Nonexistent Objects* constitute his own conjecture as to the most plausible theory of nonexistence. There is the fur- ther stage of evaluating his theory against others; this is something he does not himself undertake but like any such process it will presumably employ the standard criteria of the orthodox tradition—simplicity, scope, and so on. This evaluation, he remarks, might require "years of use and critical examination."[11] In conceiving methodological is- sues in this way Parsons is adopting Quinean notions of theoretical investigation, ones encapsulated in the phrase "inference to the best explanation" and best exemplified in the physical sciences. Nevertheless, an account of fictional, dreamed, and mythical objects along these lines has unac- ceptable consequences.

Consider now how this account applies to our old friend Sherlock Holmes. We read stories about him, discuss him with others, compare him with fictional and real detec- tives, and occasionally find it appropriate to explain to someone that "Holmes does not really exist, he is ficti- tious." There is absolutely nothing in these activities to suggest in the slightest way that they are inappropriate to Holmes. In particular, the nonexistence of Holmes seems as certain as anything could be. Parsons does not deny any of this; he begins with the hypothesis that Holmes is rea- sonably taken to be a nonexistent object on the ground that our beliefs about Holmes seem to commit us to such a thing. Problems for Parsons begin, not with his admission

10 Parsons, *Nonexistent Objects*, pp. 32–37.
11 Ibid., p. 37.

of Holmes as nonexistent, but with his classification of this view itself as a *hypothesis* that needs further testing and which, by implication, could turn out to be false. The difficulty I point out concerns the situation obtaining should this, the falsity of the supposition that Holmes does not exist, be the result finally arrived at. Parsons is strongly suggesting that such will not be the final result; nevertheless, his methodological stand implies that it might be. The point I want to press is that there is no conceivable state of affairs corresponding to the rejection of "Holmes does not exist" and hence that this sentence is not plausibly taken as a hypothesis. The consequence is that Parsons's methodological stance is revealed as misconceived.

Let us begin with the question of just how the situation corresponding to the rejection of the negative existential is to be described, given Parsons's (excellent) reasons for rejecting paraphrases of statements about the nonexistent and other such standard moves. If the hypothesis that Holmes is nonexistent is to be rejected and yet cannot be replaced with a paraphrase, what state of affairs now obtains? The original sentence was ostensibly about something, Holmes, now denied to be nonexistent; is the correct view then that Holmes is an existent object? This seems hardly acceptable in itself, and even if some general account were proposed putting Holmes (and all the other fictions, myths, and dreamed objects) among the existent, the distinctions currently made between Holmes and real things would have to be maintained and this would in effect reintroduce the classification of Holmes as nonexistent. Yet if making Holmes an existent object is not an option, and the language containing a commitment to Holmes is not to be tampered with, there hardly seems any acceptable description of the situation where it is denied that Holmes does not exist. Would it be held that "Holmes" does not have reference? This suggestion would conflict with other views Parsons holds about the implausibility of denying the commitments of names in fiction, and it would conflict also with what has been said about reference in earlier chapters. So, given Parsons's other views about paraphrase and reference, it looks as if the "hypotheses" that Parsons implies could be rejected really cannot be—and if not, it cannot be counted as a hypothesis at all but as some sort of logical truth. And if this is right, then it is a misconception to take a theory of fictional objects as comparable to a theory in physics or chemistry, one revisable in the light of future data. In the case of nonexistent objects, we have no conception of what the replacing theory could be.[12]

There is another objection to Parsons's methodology: it is unclear what the "data and other theories," to which accounts of nonexistent objects must conform, can be. Here "data" is the more basic consideration, for presumably the "other theories" are ones that concern this data; so that if the plausibility of an appeal to data is undermined then theories that make this appeal are thereby rendered otiose. Given Parsons's remarks on the relations between dream reports and dream experiences, it seems reasonable to suppose that the data he has in mind as corresponding to assertions about fictions are inner experiences. But as indicated above, there are few such experiences for reports about fictions. Possibly this data is the behavior of people who read and talk about stories—but this interpretation makes for a considerable disanalogy with dream reports with which

12 Perhaps the reply might be that on a Quinean outlook *any* theory is replaceable if enough rearrangements in the surrounding framework are made, and so in principle is "Holmes does not exist." My point is that, given Parsons's other semantical views, we have no idea what such a rearranged theoretical situation would be like. Even if one accepts the (quite implausible) Quinean stance here, the problems in finding a suitable description of the possible state in question seem to indicate that statements about Holmes's existence have much the conceptual status of those in mathematics and logic, which seems enough to declassify them with theories in the physical sciences.

Parsons compares remarks about fictions, and it amounts
to giving up the Quinean standpoint of accepting theory on
the basis of simplifying experience. At the very least, we
are due an accounting of this data; lacking this, one is entitled find Parsons's appeal to data here unconvincing.

A defender of Parsons's procedures might feel that I am
being too hard on him. After all, there is disagreement
about the status of nonexistent objects—the current po-
lemics, itself merely a skirmish in a long series of battles
begun with Russell's assault on Meinong, being a case in
point. Surely Parsons is thinking of these discussions when
he speaks of "other theories"; he is even offering the opti-
mistic opinion that such debates can be settled—even if it
does take years. Now this response is a reasonable one, and
after all I should not give the impression of not respecting
the work of a fellow Meinongian even if he has gone in a
very different direction from that I have myself taken.
What then of all this theorizing? There are, of course, many
potential contributions to a correct account among the theoretical discussions of this century. The characterization
Parsons has offered, however, that a correct such theory
"simplifies reports of our experiences" in the way dream
reports are supposed to, does not describe the aims of these
theories in any natural way. These debates are, basically,
semantical or conceptual ones concerned with meaning or
analyses of particular concepts. There is nothing analogous
to dream experiences with which these deal. Parsons is
right in thinking that any successful theory of nonexistent
objects must be related to these other discussions in an appropriate way and that evaluating proposals will be a difficult and lengthy process. Nevertheless, the issues are basically conceptual and so not governed by Quinean criteria
of theory acceptance; these criteria are taken from the empirical sciences and not applicable to the conceptual analyses and clarifications that a study of fiction demands.
Yet if I am right about this characterization, there is no

reason to think that there will not ultimately be agreement—here Parsons's hopeful and tolerant attitude can certainly be maintained.

At this point I consider a somewhat different methodological line that might appear to suit Parsons's requirements. He does not himself propose this; indeed, it runs counter to motivations that are important to him. Even so, it is appropriate to consider it since it seems to meet some of the difficulties just raised while continuing to locate the project of rehabilitating nonexistent objects within Parsons's orthodox tradition; and it is illuminating to see what the consequences of this alternative proposal are for his enterprise. The methodological stance I have in mind is the revisionary or eliminationist perspective Quine adopts toward belief in ordinary objects which is frequently advocated in (for example) the philosophy of mind. Parsons implies that Holmes's nonexistence might have to be rejected, but at the same time this rejection cannot appeal to paraphrases of sentences about Holmes or to other standard means of eliminating prima facie commitments to nonexistent objects. An eliminationist might suggest that the appropriate perspective is that current language about nonexistent objects constitutes a primitive and unsophisticated theory of such things, or at least that there is a primitive theory embodied in current talk. Careful investigation may well yield a better, more accurate account that would allow the replacement of current idioms for the nonexistent by more suitable terminology. This kind of linguistic revision has occurred in various fields investigated in science—for example, folk theories of disease as resulting from humors or magic have now been replaced by accounts in terms of microbes—so why should not this be possible with nonexistent objects? Indeed, at one time Russell expressed thinking much like this with regard to his theory of descriptions (see Chapter 1). This view would give Parsons what he needs, a rationale whereby current talk of nonexistent objects is rejected wholesale yet without invoking paraphrase or pretense proposals, and it would fit with his notion of years of testing. Could Parsons think of his project in this way?

As noted, Parsons himself never entertains such an idea, perhaps because he does not want to weaken his prima facie evidence for nonexistence, the currency of language apparently denoting the nonexistent. But apart from this, there is a decisive objection to the eliminationist's conception of the nonexistence issue in that it includes a conceptual absurdity. There is no subject matter of fiction apart from fictional discourse as we practice it; to identify the nonexistent objects Parsons wants to theorize about one has to use just the current referential idioms of fiction. To suppose that the names and definite descriptions currently used in referring to fictional characters are inaccurate and do not pick out their subject matter as well as some other possible vocabulary, or that the sentences ("Holmes smokes a pipe") currently employed to make claims about them fit the data less well than others, is just logically incoherent. How could anything refer to Sherlock Holmes better than "Sherlock Holmes" or state what "Holmes smokes a pipe" states better than this sentence itself? In the physical sciences there is a set of phenomena independent of language or theory and against which proposed hypotheses can be tested. But that is not true here, where to identify the subject matter under discussion one can only employ the very vocabulary which on the current suggestion is subject to elimination. An eliminationist procedure does not fit the problem of nonexistence, then. This failure casts further doubt on Parsons's Quinean methodology, for it that were appropriate then revision or elimination should be a possible methodological perspective. These reflections seem to me to fortify the outlook I have been affirming: issues within the general problem of nonbeing have to do with language, reference, and meaning and can only be settled by getting conceptual matters straight. And when they are straightened out, nonexistent objects turn out not to be independent of the language used about them.

But if Quinean methodology does not offer the proper viewpoint for understanding Parsons's work, what does? Parsons himself points out that his claim that there are nonexistent objects could be taken as a contribution to descriptive metaphysics: it could be suggested "that I have been describing the everyday beliefs of everyday people without philosophical training, and pointing out that these beliefs involve a commitment to nonexistent things."[13] Perhaps Parsons would be willing to accept this characterization as far as it goes. Yet he recognizes that some philosophers would feel that, even if ordinary belief is committed to nonexistent objects, there is the further and (for them) more interesting question of whether there really are such things. For Parsons too this is a genuine issue, albeit one on which "probably very little of substance can be said at this point."[14] Indeed, earlier he had called debate on this topic "fruitless."[15]

I have just been arguing that Parsons's commitment to nonexistent objects cannot be justified on straightforward Quinean grounds. If he wants some other status than descriptive metaphysics for his project, what can this be? One possibility is to see it in terms of Carnap's methodological stance, which Parsons is interested in and presents without explicit adoption or rejection. For Carnap a question of the form, Are there really things of such and such a sort? is a pseudoquestion that calls for a decision rather than an investigation, in this case the decision "whether or not to adopt a language that uses quantifier idioms" in connection with nonexistent objects. Parsons is sympathetic to a

13 Parsons, "Are There Nonexistent Objects?" p. 370.
14 Ibid., p. 370.
15 Parsons, Nonexistent Objects, p. 206.

positive choice here; from this standpoint, "many philosophers are wrong in thinking they have good reasons for rejecting a form of language that other people use with comfort."[16] From this Carnapian perspective there are nonexistent objects because everyday discourse includes expressions that take the nonexistent as their denotata. This language has simply been adopted by ordinary speakers and used "with comfort." Parsons's formal semantics can be regarded as an attempt to regiment the idioms of everyday fictional discourse, and his view that there are nonexistent objects as simply reflecting their acceptance in common language. So interpreted, there is no conflict between Parsons's position and the account I am offering, itself an exercise in descriptive metaphysics. There might well be a conflict in how the details go, but we would be agreeing that the theories we are offering intend to reflect the commitments of common speech. Yet if Parsons's position is taken in this way, there is no place for the further question, Are there really nonexistent objects? since this is answered from the Carnapian standpoint simply by noting that a decision has been made to accept them. And further, there is nothing to be gained by years of use and critical examination, for the issue is not a theoretical one which extensive investigation could settle. Parsons's supposition that lengthy testing is in order and his disinclination to adopt wholeheartedly Carnap's stand swings his conception of the methodology underpinning his project away from the defensible and sound one here, as I see it, toward the objectionable Quinean one discussed earlier.

This has been a rather long excursion into methodology, but the stakes are large ones, and I think enough has been said to cast serious doubt on the idea that support for a

16 Parsons, "Are There Nonexistent Objects?" p. 370. Carnap's views are given in Rudolph Carnap, "Empiricism, Semantics and Ontology," in *Meaning and Necessity* (Chicago: University of Chicago Press, 1956).

Meinongian view can rest ultimately on the kinds of consideration Quine recommends: that accepting nonexistent objects is justified because in the long run this may turn out to be the result of inference to the best explanation. If I am right, this counts against the appropriateness of this concept of philosophizing in general: philosophical theorizing is not governed by the standards of theory construction in the empirical sciences but has its own procedures, of which a central one is conceptual analysis.

ARE THERE REALLY NONEXISTENT OBJECTS?

The preceding discussion has raised an important issue not explicitly addressed heretofore—whether, apart from matters of descriptive or revisionary analysis, there really are nonexistent objects. This question is answered from the perspective of the present account in much the same way as it is for Carnap: there really are such things in that we do in fact talk about them. They are an accepted part of our conceptual scheme. As I have indicated, societies that do not accept such objects are imaginable; still, it seems to me extremely unlikely that such societies exist for the tendency to make up characters and tell and enjoy stories about them is surely among the universal traits of mankind. But even if there should be such societies, this would not alter the fact that nonexistent objects are a part of the conceptual scheme I am clarifying.

Some philosophers (as Parsons has noted) would not find this kind of answer satisfying. They would contend that, even if common speech is committed to nonexistent objects, one can still wonder whether there really are such things. What is to be said about this question? The first issue to raise, what exactly does it ask? Is it asking whether, over and above the commitments of common discourse, there genuinely are merely grammatical objects of the sort I have claimed fictional characters to be? It is hard to see what sense there could be to this question, for conceptual objects just are ones corresponding to uses of referring expressions and have no status apart from this usage. So the question must concern objects conceived as having the status of Being or subsistence. Given this notion, the question becomes, are there really, apart from the commitments of language, entities having Being or subsistence? Now I cannot claim to have proved that there cannot be such things or that "Being" and "subsistence" are incoherent notions; rather, I have attempted to show that common usage—at least the everyday language of fiction—does not carry a commitment to such states and that the standard philosophical arguments for them are inadequate. It might be held that that these conclusions, even if correct, do not rule out the possibility of good arguments presenting a plausible case for subsistence. This is correct; in some sense, the possibility of subsistent objects remains. Nevertheless, this is a very weak possibility at best, at least where literary fictions are concerned, for if my analysis has been sound there are no practical grounds at all for holding even that there might be persuasive arguments for fictional subsistent objects. The possibility of such things is bare indeed.

The question of whether there are really such things as nonexistent objects may, however, be given a different meaning: will final scientific theory assume them? will our best scientific account of the world "in the long run" assume that there are subsisting but not existing entities? Indeed it is possible that the question in this form was partly what Parsons had in mind when he mentioned global considerations and years of use and critical examination. There is this much to be said in favor of the speculation that science might actually come to the assumption that there are such things: it is practically impossible to predict what sci-

entific theories will assume. Who could have anticipated
the remarkable consequences of relativistic physics with
its unification of space, time, matter, and energy? or the
bizarre conceptual consequences of quantum mechanics for
notions of objectivity and causality? or the strange proposals taken seriously by contemporary physicists such as
antimatter and the ramified universes discussed in contemporary cosmology? It does not seem to me altogether impossible that science might come to assume subsistent objects—although it is hard to imagine just what role such
objects could play in theories about full concrete reality.
Still, in view of the conceptual innovations of twentieth-
century physics particularly, this possibility cannot be entirely ruled out. Does this vindicate Parsons's speculation?
In a measure perhaps, but then it is important to notice
that the possibility lies in future developments in science,
not in investigations in metaphysics, semantics, analyses
of usage, or proposals in formal logic. If the arguments presented in this study are sound, there are no reasons within
these fields requiring the assumption of subsistent entities
as opposed to what I have called merely conceptual ones. It
follows that it is not philosophers who can make the case
for nonexistent yet subsistent entities, but scientists.
These entities would then be assumed in important but
highly technical disciplines remote from ordinary references to the kinds of objects around which philosophical
studies of nonbeing have turned. The status of Sherlock
Holmes, the golden mountain, and the round square would
not be affected by these scientific developments, should
they occur.

The question of whether subsistent objects really occur
might take a more anthropological form: are there societies
where such objects are assumed, even if we do not assume
them in ours? Could there be a society for which a descriptive metaphysician could correctly claim that subsistent
objects are accepted in that society? This suggestion seems

comparable to that above about possible future science, and the response must be comparable as well. Nothing I have said provides grounds for ruling out a priori such a possibility, for it seems conceivable that there should be a society about which, when its beliefs and linguistic practices became fully articulated, we would be inclined to say that its members accepted subsistent objects. Yet, while this bare possibility must remain open perhaps, it is extremely difficult to imagine the concrete beliefs and practices that would make this description appropriate. If this were a society having beliefs differing from those characteristic of Western society, the most likely candidates for this status would be connected with religion or cosmology. We would probably find ourselves classifying objects of such beliefs as existing—existing in some unfamiliar realm, heaven, or hell, or in some strange form, but existing nevertheless. The circumstances under which we would find it appropriate to classify these objects as subsisting, not fully existing but not nonexisting either or being purely abstract, are hard to imagine. Still, in view of the innumerable classifications and ontological categories available, and the variety of contextual situations in which these categories might be employed, once again it seems unjustified to rule out subsistent objects altogether.

A large part of the problem is the notion of "subsistence" (or "Being") itself. At least one of the principal motivations for introducing this notion was to account for the use of names and other referring expressions that denote literary fictions. Objects so denoted were supposed to have some form of existence even if not concrete actuality. My view is that this is wrongheaded; there is no need for such a notion. So at this point, trying to make sense of the question, Could there really be subsistent entities? we are in the position of trying to find employment for a notion invoked for a largely misconceived purpose. This does not require that the notion have no meaning whatever, but it certainly puts the burden of giving an analysis of it whereby it has a possible application on those who want to employ it. This is no easy task, for the natural explanation of the concept, that is, the status in reality fictional characters have, includes a misconception. Perhaps there are explanations that do not include this misconception, but then it is up to the friends of subsistent objects to provide them, and perhaps those of us not at this point privy to these explanations can be excused for being skeptical whether there are any such things. Lacking any original grounds for assigning the concept, we must find the task of giving it further applications obscure to the point of being entirely senseless. It is not surprising that it is difficult to give a direct answer to the question of whether there are really nonexistent objects apart from what common linguistic practice assumes. Still, even in the light of these considerations, the earlier conclusion still stands: it is not completely unthinkable that there should be a society accepting subsistent objects, for it is impossible to anticipate what principles might be adopted in alien or futuristic situations. Yet even if some society were to be judged to do this, the remarks made about analogous developments in science hold here as well. The objects so countenanced would not be Sherlock Holmes, the golden mountain, or the round square as we conceive them, but items that would be extremely strange to us and not locateable in our conceptual scheme.

6

REAL THINGS IN FICTION,
LOGICAL COMPLETENESS, AND
OTHER FORMS OF REPRESENTATION

The position developed in the previous chapters can be applied to various troublesome philosophical issues. One of these stems from the appearance in fiction of names and descriptions of historical individuals and places: are there references to real things in fiction? Another concerns logical completeness: since characters are described to only a limited extent in their stories, does it follow that they have only the features they are said to have? If so, they are logically incomplete, neither possessing nor failing to possess many normal attributes. These two problems are related, in that examining the former yields results useful for dealing with the latter. This discussion sets the stage for a look at the relation of realistic fiction to other forms of representation incorporating nonexistent objects—dreams, myths, ghost stories, and modes outside the mainstream Western literary tradition.

ARE STORIES ABOUT REAL THINGS?

As in previous chapters, I am primarily concerned here with realistic fiction, but I also make a few remarks on other types. It is a familiar fact about the genres making up this kind of fiction that authors write their works against a background taken over from actuality. The Holmes stories are *set*, as we say, in the London of the late nineteenth century. That fiction should have a historical setting is practically a necessity for it to function in our culture. If authors had to introduce explicitly each fact pertaining to a scene, their writing would become immensely cumbersome; or else, to avoid this, they would make fictional situations extremely spare (if under these conditions fiction was possible at all). In either case, literature could not then have its present function of giving easily comprehended depictions of human figures performing familiar actions in lifelike contexts. The problem is dealt with through a convention whereby characters are to be understood as occurring against a factual setting filling out a scene being depicted. Readers take it that Holmes, described as a man with certain features and in such and such a situation, lives in a certain social setting the historical features of which we are broadly familiar. A general understanding of history enables us to know what to expect in a story regarding dress, social arrangements, technology, forms of speech, and the like; we do not have to be told explicitly. Conventions of setting and background make the author's task vastly easier to the point of making it possible at all. Various aesthetic purposes are served as well. A certain kind of background conveys a particular mood or leads readers to expect particular kinds of event (think of Gothic novels, where the setting is a sure indication of the action to follow), and certain types of context highlight specific emotions or themes (recall beginnings typical of romances or adventure stories). That fictional events take place in a setting is not only a practical and perhaps logical necessity for fictional discourse but also an aesthetic contribution.

In giving a story specific historical background, an author is not committed to the inclusion in the contents of every detail of this background. If authors were to accept such a commitment, they would be writing history, not fiction, for there would be no created characters and events drawn from the imgination. Readers are interested in Holmes's adventures without worrying whether the figures and events described correspond to anything historical. Fiction tells a story located in a setting taken over to the extent that it suits the purposes of the writing; it is not journalism or history to be judged by its correspondence to fact. A clear case is 221B Baker Street: like Conan Doyle we all know that, as far as the real London goes, no detective lived there and we find this perfectly acceptable. Even if there were a major variation from history, this need not be a flaw, for artistic purposes might be served by changing the distance between one place and another or altering the time of a historical event. On the other hand, in certain contexts variation from historical fact would be a slip;[1] the assumption is that accurate reflection of the facts is important to the artistic merits of the writing. How much divergence between real circumstance and fictional setting is acceptable varies with types of fiction. Historical novels or fictionalized biography must be more or less true to the known facts, and major variations are mistakes; authors in this genre usually do research and often before publication submit their manuscripts to experts to avoid factual errors. Gothic romances, on the other hand, assume no actual setting and are vague as to particular time and locale; they require no historical research but only a familiarity with the conventions of romantic literature. In these and indeed in all genres of fiction there is the constraint of plausibility. This constraint functions differently for different types of literature. To have the action in a romance punctuated by the kinds of large-scale historical event which

---

1 "Former members of the eight-person fact-checking department [of the *New Yorker* magazine] said that they were even asked to check facts in poetry and works of fiction, verifying, for instance, that street names in short stories were accurate if the town was a real one"; *Los Angeles Times*, June 20, 1984, pt. I, p. 10.

occur in Tolstoy's novels would detract from the emotional
force characteristic of such tales, and immerse it all its desire
to be immersed in the emotional details of a relationship
would be frustrated by such interruptions. Historical fiction, on the other hand, cannot be so confined but typically
covers broad movements and long stretches of time. Similarly, what is appropriate for detective stories will not do
for novels of manners. Different kinds of fiction suit different kinds of interest and conventions, for background content varies accordingly. But the major point here is that
suitability is not in general decided simply by considerations of faithfulness to historical fact; rather, this is a matter of the purposes of a given mode of fiction and the conventions it incorporates reflecting them.

   This point I believe resolves an issue discussed by David
Lewis.[2] In "The Adventure of the Speckled Band," Holmes

---

2 David Lewis, "Truth in Fiction," reprinted in *Philosophical Papers*,
Vol. I (New York: Oxford University Press, 1983), pp. 261–280. Lewis
offers a view whereby "reasoning about truth in fiction is very like counterfactual reasoning" (p. 269). This view seems wrong to me for several
reasons. First, as I have argued at length, creatures in fiction are not real
ones subject to considerations of genuine possibility but created, merely
grammatical objects that could not appear in the real world. To claim that
fictional characters could exist in some possible world—that they might
exist—would be like claiming that the average American as such could be
talked to or live in a certain house. Second, fictional worlds can contain
contradictions. Lewis recognizes this and tries to deal with it; nevertheless, he holds that where the impossibility is blatant (e.g., where someone
squares the circle) then anything whatever is true in the fiction (pp. 274–
275). This does not seem right; even in a story where someone squares the
circle, not *everything* goes—it is a circle that is squared and not a triangle,
for example. The logic of real possibility need not apply in all types of
fiction; logical principles may themselves vary through different genres.
Third, Lewis holds that a storyteller is pretending to report known fact—a
view criticized earlier (see Chapter 2). A storyteller is pretending only in
the sense that he or she is talking about a set of situations that did not
actually occur. The objects described are not genuinely possible ones but
belong to the category of conceptual constructions; they are not contingently nonexistent but unreal. There are other versions of the possible-
world treatment of fiction; all are I think subject to difficulties of these

solves the mystery by pointing out that the victim was killed by a Russell's viper that had to climb a rope in order to reach him. In fact, a Russell's viper is not able to climb ropes, so commentators have claimed that either the case remains open or the snake reached its victim in some other way. Lewis does not accept this claim, but he notes that it reflects the principle that what is true in a fiction is what is true in the actual world taken as background for a story. Lewis goes on to suggest a second and conflicting principle, that what is true in a story is what is true according to what the community for which the story is intended believes about the historical situation taken as setting. Conan Doyle's readers believed (or at least were willing to accept) that Russell's vipers did climb ropes. Lewis does not try to decide between these principles, but it seems to me that the proper judgment is that which convention is appropriate depends on the particular genre of fiction in question. Since Conan Doyle's readers did not reject the solution as given in the story, it is plausible to say that for detective stories Lewis's second principle is the one that holds in actual practice. On the other hand, there might be types of writing—for instance, historical fiction clearly intended to be exactly faithful to reality—for which strict adherence to fact is required; in such cases the first principle would be correct. What is true in fiction can vary with genre and no one general principle of content holds.

We are now in a position to consider the issue of the status of real people who appear in stories. Suppose that Conan Doyle had written that Gladstone has tea with Holmes (to use John Woods's example). Does the real Gladstone appear in the stories: does the name "Gladstone" in

---

sorts. Further criticism of this position is offered by John Woods, "Animadversions and Open Questions, Reference, Inference and Truth in Fiction," *Poetics* 11 (1982):558, and by Robert Howell, "Fictional Objects: How They Are and How They Aren't," *Poetics* 8 (1979):175.

the text of the story refer to the actual, historical person?
Considerations about background are pertinent here. Conan Doyle has taken nineteenth-century England as his setting and has created a character based on an individual, the
historical Gladstone, who existed in this setting. Particular
characters taken over from real life, or story locations
taken over from the general background, are to be explained in terms of the principle that fiction takes place in
a setting. Such figures or places appearing in a story are
created by an author using the circumstances history provides to supply details. References in a literary text are governed by the "in the story" operator and do not purport to
be about the actual man but only about his conceptual
counterpart. A biography of Gladstone would not mention
his having tea with Holmes; at most it might note that a
fictionalized Gladstone appeared in a work by Conan Doyle
and was said there to have tea. On the other hand, a biography of Holmes, having to rely solely on the contents of
stories and not reality, would include the Gladstone meeting.[3] Again, minor facts about the real Gladstone could be
altered for purposes of the narrative. Gladstone could be
made slightly older or younger than his actual age, for example, and if so he would simply be that way "in the
story." The principle of poetic license is a familiar one.
Since Conan Doyle's basic intention is to tell a story rather
than to present history slightly fictionalized, he must be
faithful to historical circumstances only to the extent that
he maintains plausibility. If one of his sentences about
Gladstone misrepresented his actual age and was subject to
criticism, the reason would not be that it is false, for
Conan Doyle is not writing news. It would be instead that
the sentence offends the reader's sense of verisimilitude—
the discrepancy is enough to affect plausibility and a reader

3 See John Woods, "Fictionality and the Logic of Relations," *Southern
Journal of Philosophy* 7 (1969):57.

is made to lose absorption in the narrative. Minor divergencies from fact tend not to be noticed or to be unimportant if they are; major ones tend to be distracting. In extreme and continued cases of divergence, one would question an author's competence or perhaps begin to revise one's classification of a work; what looked like a historical novel might be turning out to be fantasy, horror, or science fiction. Certainly if matters reach this stage the author has failed in his or her prima facie purpose of interesting and entertaining an audience—unless the effect actually achieved has itself been intended. In any case, faithfulness or unfaithfulness to historical facts does not in itself constitute a merit or flaw in fiction. The appearance in stories of names and descriptions of actual people and places is not evidence that these works are about real, historical things.

But if historical names appearing in fiction do not denote actual individuals but only their created counterparts, how is that we can learn real history from fiction? The answer is that in such cases there is the presumption that the character has essentially the features of the actual person; descriptions in the story are expected to preserve verisimilitude. Readers understand that a story is told against a background of historical circumstance which is broadly mirrored in the contents of the narrative. When we read about Parisian society in Proust or English family life in Jane Austen, we take ourselves to be reading about events characteristic of actual historical situations. This explains why one can learn about other societies and times through reading fiction even though the primary intention of such authors as Proust and Austen is not to report or inform. These considerations might be summed up this way: in the strict sense specified in Chapter 2, names in the text of a work of fiction refer to the characters and places as set out in the work itself—to the conceptual objects that constitute fiction—and the sentences including them have as truth conditions the contents of the work. Nevertheless,

because of conventions relating novelistic contents and
historical setting, facts can be recorded in fiction and information conveyed by it; hence it is natural to say in a
broader sense that a story is about a real person or an actual
locale. Here the referent is a fiction-as-representing-a-real-
thing, and truth conditions for assertions are not merely
sayso but sayso-as-reflecting-reality.

These considerations are central to an explanation of literary genres such as satire, moralistic fiction, social criticism, and humorous and ironical commentary. The issue
can be put à la Kant: given the distinction between factual
circumstances taken as background and created story content, and given also that a story is not to be taken as a
transcription of reality, how are these types of literature
possible? The explanation lies in the principle given above.
Such genres are made possible through general acceptance
of the convention that story content can be based on reality. To understand a novel or play as satire is to assume
that the author has based the story on real-life individuals;
it is to assume further that the author intends that the
story be recognized as so based and thus that the events
and suggested evaluations in the fiction are to be projected
back onto their real counterparts. Satire and the other literary forms mentioned depend on the transparency of the
fact that a given character is based on a particular real individual; having so created a character, an author is in position to deliver a satirical message through the features and
actions ascribed to that character. There are familiar ways
of achieving this transparency, typically through writing
the subject's major personal features and social or historical situation into the fiction. Accordingly, matters of libel
or slander become relevant, and to protect themselves authors often add a disclaimer such as the familiar "characters included are not based on real people living or dead and
any simililarity is purely coincidental." Writing is slan-
derous if it attributes certain kinds of action or motive to a

real person by way of a fictional counterpart, but questions of slander or libel have to be settled on a case-by-case basis that takes into account circumstances of a work's composition and contents. That there are such things as disclaimers does not imply that an author writes directly about a historical individual. Indeed, they can be seen as implying that this is not the case, for in denying that a set of characters is based on real individuals a disclaimer makes it explicit that for the particular type of fiction in question the relation between accounts of characters and corresponding real individuals is that of being *based on* rather than that of *reporting*.

A related problem is the classification of particular literary works: is a piece satire or simply storytelling? are the events depicted to be understood as symbolic or just as good entertainment? These matters are notoriously difficult, partly because of the problem of ascertaining an author's intentions but also because of the different levels of interpretion possible. There is, for example, historical fiction, defined by the notion of a set of characters based on more or less recognizable historical individuals. Yet there is no intention to conform to actual history; an author has considerable latitude as to what is acceptable in the fiction. In practice, historical fiction is difficult to distinguish from fictionalized history, where the goal is to represent faithfully the actual facts and only to fill in what adds to an appreciation of history. An author of fictionalized history who does not report the facts fails; the sentences in such history can be judged true or false on the basis of history. To give prominence to the sayso criterion and to insist on a distinction between what happens in the story and what really occurs would violate the underlying intention of informing. Here the notion of being based on has given way to that of representing. No doubt there are works for which it is uncertain whether an author means to be representing history or creating entertaining scenes based on history, or

for which author's intentions seem too indefinite for classification. Perhaps there are works about historical situations resisting this distinction altogether. The categories of
literary classification are fluid and open-ended and may not
readily apply to given instances.

ARE FICTIONAL CHARACTERS
LOGICALLY COMPLETE?

Current opinion about whether fictional characters are logically complete is reported by Parsons: "A character created in a piece of fiction is typically incomplete, whereas
real people are complete. This seems to be the accepted
view in the literature."[4] The generally accepted standard of
completeness is as follows:[5]

> An object x is complete if it is logically true that, for any prop-
> erty P, either x has P ("x is P" is true) or x has the complement
> of P ("x is non-P" is true).

To put it informally and as it applies to some applicable
property, x is complete with respect to P if either x is P or x
is non-P. Let me elaborate the reasoning behind the claim
of incompleteness. One tells what properties a fictional
character has by looking to the contents of his story: a
character has those properties he is explicitly mentioned as
having or can readily be inferred to have from textual information. There are, however, many normal properties for
which the possession of neither the property nor its com-

---

4 Terence Parsons, *Nonexistent Objects* (New Haven, Conn.: Yale University Press, 1980), p. 184.

5 See the similar statement of the principle in Karel Lambert, *Meinong
and the Principle of Independence: Its Place in Meinong's Theory of Objects and Its Significance in Contemporary Philosophical Logic* (Cambridge: Cambridge University Press, 1983), p. 26.

plement is indicated. A text can describe a character just so far; inevitably there are many features on which it is silent. This is so even if a work is extremely detailed, for no fiction could possibly address all the logically appropriate properties for any fictional item. It follows that for an unaddressed property the character neither has it nor lacks it; hence this character is incomplete with respect to such a feature. Clearly there are many properties of this type. Does Holmes have a mole on his left shoulder? Conan Doyle does not say. In addition to Holmes's mole, there is the matter of a scar on his thigh, his grandmother's birthplace, his violin teacher's maiden name, what he had for dinner last evening, and so on. Characters are only what they are stated or immediately implied to be, which leaves them, logically speaking, quite gappy indeed.[6]

In this section I look at various considerations that might be thought to supplement this reasoning, but first let us consider the principles holding for fictional characters as defined by their basic conceptual status, items to be regarded from the "in the story" standpoint. From this logical perspective, objects are to be regarded as governed by all the logical and physical principles that govern real things—or anyway are believed by the intended audience to govern them, if Lewis's second principle is (sometimes) correct. Among these principles is logical completeness, since real entities are conceived as logically complete. Inside a work of fiction, objects—normal objects such as people and tables and trees—are logically complete. Another way of seeing this is to recall that, for Watson, whose conceptual station is definitive of the inside standpoint, Holmes is not incomplete with respect to a mole on his shoulder. Watson would suppose—it is part of our understanding of a character to conceive him as supposing—that Holmes was per-

---

6 See Parsons, *Nonexistent Objects*, pp. 183–184, for such a line of thought.

fectly normal logically speaking and either has a mole or does not. Watson would certainly not think of Holmes as logically incomplete with respect to moles (or anything else); the principle of completeness would be part of what constitutes Watson's outlook. He realizes that his friend is remarkable, but not in *that* way. In fact, it would be quite bizarre for Holmes to be regarded in the stories as logically incomplete—for Holmes to be understood in the stories as neither having a mole nor failing to, neither having a Cornish grandmother nor not having one, neither having a second violin nor lacking one, and so on. This would leave Holmes such a conceptually odd figure that he would not be logically fit to play the role of the protagonist in a series of detective stories, the role of a normal human being with exceptional mental abilities. Despite the fact that certain human features are ascribed to him, he would not qualify as a normal person, for persons are logically complete. He would be a logically skeletal figure, having a few properties against a huge background of conceptual emptiness. To make Holmes incomplete *in the story*, then, would render him conceptually unsuitable for the role of a character in ordinary narrative fiction. Indeed, in the stories Holmes is a real person and so logically complete. The claim of incompleteness ignores the principles definitive of the "in the story" context.

The issue can be approached from the other side, by comparing a standard fictional object with something that is genuinely incomplete, a Meinongian golden mountain, for example. This object ex hypothesi has only the two properties of being a mountain and being golden; it is incomplete with respect to any other property. Let us try to make this into a standard fictional object by putting it into a story. Here it is: "Once upon a time there was a golden mountain." A promising opening perhaps, but alas this must be the entire content of the story, for no other (nontrivial) story content could be added without violating the initial restriction on properties. So the golden mountain must exist in splendid logical isolation, alone in its tale. This point brings out the logical differences between incomplete objects, as philosophers have conceived them, and the typical item in fiction. An author limited to objects restricted in Meinong's way would find it impossible to produce normal fiction. The normal mode of composition is not so restricted: an author begins with an idea of a certain character and then goes on to describe her in new ways limited only by such considerations as plausibility of character development, suitability to plot, and faithfulness to background. Such practical literary constraints have nothing to do with the kinds of restriction entering into the logician's notion of an incomplete object. Again, we have the conclusion that there is a clear sense in which objects in fiction are not incomplete.

In the story, then, objects (of realistic fiction) are complete; that is, they obey this principle:

(A) In the story x is P or non-P

for any x and logically applicable P. But what of the considerations given at the beginning of this section? What principle do they show that fictions violate if it is not (A)? The argument for incompleteness was that works describe their characters only partially and do not indicate possession or nonpossession for many features. So it appears that this is the principle that fictions fail:

(B) In a story x is indicated to be P or in the story x is indicated to be non-P

(where "indicates" means "explicitly states or clearly implies"). This principle asserts that every applicable property is actually stated or implied to hold for every object in a story. Principle (B) is plausibly the principle sought for,

since it concerns what is stated in the fiction, not the logical principles in force inside the fiction, and it was a defi-
ciency in mentioning features that led to the appearance of
incompleteness. But (B) is plainly false for objects in fiction; for each object there are many properties whose application is not indicated one way or the other.

Perhaps a way of stating the worry of proponents of the
incompleteness thesis is this: if fictional writing violates
(B), how can it produce objects that satisfy (A)? Fictions are
constructed by their descriptions. How can one go from descriptions inevitably partial to logically complete constructions? This perplexity is resolved once it is realized that
the creation of characters in realistic fiction is done against
a background of historical fact and logical assumption. We
read a novel with the presumption that lifelike individuals
are being described; the personal attributes, situation, and
events ascribed to them are to be regarded as indicative of
the general situation in which they are to be located. They
are to be understood as having all the characteristics real
people have: a normal past, a familiar human body, a realistic social situation, and the like. As objects they obey all
the laws pertaining to real people, among them logical
completeness. What is explicitly said in the fiction is to be
supplemented by attributions generated by a presumption
of normality; we take it that the individuals in the story
are normal and have the usual characteristics even though
what particular features they have is not fully specified.
Our thinking about a fictional character is in many ways
conceptually comparable to our understanding of a real per-
sonage we encounter in writing about the past, or of someone a correspondent describes having met. Exactly the
same background assumptions apply in the two sorts of
case, except that for fiction we understand that the individual is created and unreal. Fictional writing can create a realistic individual because of the contributions readers im-
port from this background; explicit description creates

against a presumed setting of normality and the objects so created must be understood as corresponding to its physical and logical features.

This explanation might not be satisfying to proponents of the incompleteness thesis, for there are a number of considerations that might appear to support the view that fictions have the more radical Meinongian incompleteness. The first of these acknowledges that Meinongian objects initially limited to a specific number of properties are not logically suitable as items in fiction. Yet this does not count against the possibility of Meinongian characters, the suggestion goes, since there is no reason why such objects have to be limited at the outset to a definite number of properties. An author simply writes a story; when it is done a number of properties have been assigned to a character, and this set of properties, however many its members, defines the Meinongian object—which is still incomplete. Now this more liberal version of Meinongianism does provide objects more in accord with the practices of authorship, but it still fails to generate an object in harmony with the rules of fictional discourse. An object produced in the above way is still necessarily incomplete in the story: although it has all the properties the story assigns it, in the story it fails to obey the principle of completeness. Watson would still find such a Holmes an exceedingly odd figure lacking many normal properties and certainly not suitable as a solver of crimes.

A second argument is based on the sayso criterion, that what is in a story is what the story says (or pretty clearly implies). Since there are many features on which a story is silent, it follows that a character is incomplete with respect to such properties; the sayso criterion supports incompleteness. The trouble with this contention is that it takes the sayso criterion in too restrictive a way. A character is to be understood as having not only the properties overtly given to her, but also those to be attributed to her

through her satisfying the conventions of fictional literature. Among these are completeness: in the story a character is to be understood as logically complete, even if the
story does not specifically indicate this (as stories typically
do not). A story "says" that its objects are complete in implying that they are; completeness is just one of the conventions constituitive of realistic fiction. A story should be
understood as "saying" not only what its sentences directly
state or entail, but also what the fact that it is a realistic
work implies. It is worth a slight digression to illustrate
this further. Consider the situation confronting a director
of a film based on a Holmes story. Many of the details to
appear in the film will not have been mentioned in the literary piece—how many items are on Holmes's desk, exactly what vehicles run through Baker Street, what shoes
Watson wears. Clearly the director would not want the
film to be somehow incomplete with respect to these matters; this would not be true to the contents of the story and
would produce a very strange film extremely different from
the normal detective movie. Rather, in such a situation a
director would fill in appropriate details on the basis of
facts about London at the time the stories are set. This fill-
ing-in would be in accord with logical completeness. The
director is not here adding to the original story itself; he or
she can be regarded as contributing to the creation of a new
work, a film, based on the literary work. But this new creation is faithful to the conceptual principles of the old and
so is logically complete. My suggestion is that the director
in creating this new work is drawing out the implied contents of the old but in so doing must obey the principles
governing the original. It is simply implicit in the story, as
part of its London setting, that there are things of a certain
type on Holmes's desk, probably horse-drawn cabs and the
like in Baker Street, and a certain style of shoe which Watson wears. The film director has occasion to make such
matters explicit since the medium requires it, but in so do-

ing the director must reflect conceptual as well as historical background. What is said in a story is in a larger sense not just what is stated by the sentences but includes the imputation of background where this (for realistic fiction) includes completeness.

A third consideration concerns verification. Suppose that some such principle as this is proposed: if there is no way in principle to verify whether P applies to x, then "x is P" is meaningless. The advocate of incompleteness might argue that sentences that attribute properties to a character are meaningless for properties on which the work is silent, for there is no way in principle to verify whether they apply. "Holmes has a mole on his left shoulder" is meaningless, since given the text of the Holmes series there is no possible way of telling whether or not having a mole is one of his properties. Since this sentence is meaningless, Holmes is incomplete with respect to moles—and the claim of incompleteness is supported. The central difficulty for this argument (apart from problems about verificationism generally, which I am ignoring) is that in the story verification holds—or, it holds there as firmly as it does in reality. Watson would certainly believe that he could find out whether Holmes had a mole—by asking him or by taking a look when Holmes was changing shirts. The principles under which we conceive Watson attribute to him the ability to check on issues such as a possible mole for his flat-mate, since these principles are the ones holding for (our) reality; we suppose that fictional characters have the same abilities to verify claims as we do. To this there might be the reply that, while *Watson* can be conceived as verifying "Holmes has a mole," *we* cannot be, as there is nothing we can conceivably do to decide whether this sentence is true or false. For us the predicate is meaningless and Holmes incomplete—even if not for Watson. This reply misconceives the nature of the issue. The question is not whether we can practically or theoretically verify some given assertion, but whether the sentences attributing the disputed predicates occur in a logical context that includes completeness. And of course the disputed sentence does occur in such a context: verification is just as much (or as little) a part of Holmes's world as it is of ours. Contrast the claim that Holmes is incomplete with respect to a mole on his shoulder with one which (in the story) Watson could not be conceived as able to verify in principle, say "The Form of the Good is the supreme Form." The case for meaninglessness is intuitively much stronger here than it is for Holmes's mole, for a verification condition is violated in a more radical way. That there is contrast between these cases shows that there is a sense in which Holmes's possible mole does not violate a normal verification principle.

A final argument that the supporter of Meinongian incompleteness might present is that there are many representations where it seems out of place, just logically inappropriate, to raise questions of further detail. Consider George Washington as portrayed on the U.S. twenty-five-cent piece. It would be ridiculous to ask what kind of shoes he is wearing, yet this situation is logically on a par with Holmes's mole, since in both cases there is a character defined to a certain extent only (the differences in medium do not matter for logical purposes) and what is logically absurd in the one case is absurd in the other. So, the objection concludes, as George Washington is incomplete with respect to footwear, Holmes is with respect to moles. I think that we should grant this objector that a comparison between fictions and pictorial representations is in general appropriate; the conceptual elements in the two media do correspond when matters are sorted out. And so this might appear to be a forceful objection. (In fact, this objection for a long time seemed persuasive to me.) The proper response is not that there is a basic difference between literary and pictorial forms of representation, for I do not believe that this is so; rather, the response is that these particular cases—realistic fiction and portraiture on a coin—must be thought of in different logical terms. The face of a national hero on a coin is intended chiefly to honor the hero and to recall his importance to the country. It is not intended to depict a factual situation into which a viewer is imaginatively to enter, and where there are other details to be wondered about and possibly filled in by some historical situation taken as background. Consider a style of pictorial representation that is comparable to narrative fiction, say seventeenth-century Dutch painting. About these depictions of everyday scenes one could certainly wonder what the individuals were drinking or what was going on in the next room. Indeed, we seem invited to ask such questions (especially about the next room). Here a distinction comparable to being (logically) inside a fiction versus being outside applies, and so for the "in the picture" context logical completeness holds as well. A scene is to be thought of as taking place in a realistic setting, with unrepresented states of affairs implied to exist off canvas and satisfying appropriate conceptual principles. In such paintings it is logically acceptable to ask about factual circumstances not explicitly depicted in the painting; these works could not generate the objection I am considering. But a portrait on a coin is not in this category, since it is simply a symbolic representation with no implication of setting or scene; it is not comparable in structure to realistic fiction.

None of these objections has given support to the more radical form of incompleteness which a classification of fictions with Meinongian incomplete objects entails. Fictitious characters are incomplete only in the sense that texts construct them just to a certain extent; this much must be granted to the supporters of incompleteness. Yet in a clear sense characters are complete in that (A) is understood to apply to them: within the story they are logically normal individuals. It might seem obvious that this is the case once it has been pointed out, but the problem lies, as with so many issues concerning fiction, in being able to sort out relations between logical considerations of divergent types.

OBJECTS IN MYTHS, DREAMS, AND NONREALISTIC FICTION

The principles characteristic of realistic art do not hold for all forms of representation. Realistic principles govern media dominated by the intention to present a world peopled by normal individuals performing familiar kinds of action; as well as the sorts of literature we have been discussing there are historical and narrative painting, classical theater, and the cinema. Logical completeness and an assumption of ordinary physical and social regularities are an essential part of the structure required for realizing these intentions. When the purpose is not storytelling or visual reproduction of a lifelike situation, however, other principles become appropriate. The aim may be to provide a symbolic representation of a type (a Greek statue of an athlete) or to portray a real individual as essentially the instantiation of a set of idealized attributes (likenesses on currency or stamps). There is no sequence of realistic events or scenes being depicted in these cases. A literary analogue would be the verbal portrayal of a historical individual as an idealized character; propagandistic and ideological literature are full of such accounts. George Washington has certainly been written up for Americans as the perfect soldier-statesman in such a way that facts about his life recede into the background and he becomes more the exemplar of virtues than a historical individual. A novelist might write out the description of a character as a preliminary to deciding whether to introduce her into the story; at this initial stage, without any setting, other characters, or plot, there is no fictional world and it would be wrong to impose the inside/outside distinction or the requirement of completeness.

Even within established modes of representation, principles characteristic of standard fiction are not always followed. Are mythical creatures logically complete, or those in science fiction, fantasy, fairy or ghost stories, or dreams? Unlike detective stories, these instances do not take a background of everyday normality. Science fiction, for example, typically has futuristic settings where laws and technology currently unknown are accepted as everyday phenomena. Here the everyday world has been augmented with futuristic science and technology but the accepted principles of logic still hold—the creatures appearing there, though exotic and unfamiliar, are logically complete. Yet this may not be true of all types of science fiction and fantasy, one consideration being that the line between what is physically and what is logically possible is not always distinct. Is time travel, one of the staples of science fiction, a conceptual or merely a physical impossibility? The issue is complicated by twentieth-century advances in physics, since if time measurement is relativized to the speed of the observer then the issue of the logical status of time travel becomes complex and obscure. Indeed, there are a number of factors that make it difficult to produce with confidence a clear case of logical incompleteness. One might think that fairy stories provide unproblematic instances; consider "Goldilocks and the Three Bears." Can one reasonably press the issue of what kind of wood made up the chair Goldilocks sat on and broke? The reasoning appropriate to realistic fiction seems out of place—that in the story there is a definite answer because if one takes the perspective of Papa Bear then the information is already at hand or can be gained just by looking at the pieces of the chair or by taking them to a knowledgeable craftsman (craftsbear?). It is not, however, so obvious that this reasoning is out of place specifically because logical completeness is not in force for such tales, since there is an alternative explanation: that the world of the small child is just not as detailed as the adult world. On this latter account the possible answers that spring to an adult's mind (pine or oak or maple) are not part of the primary child's framework. The world of the child is nonspecific and does not have the background of techni cal knowledge adults have acquired—but this is not to say that it is logically incomplete. What is in question here is not simply a contrast between immature and mature conceptions, for adults can also adopt a child's outlook (as when writing children's literature, for example). There are adult genres that raise similar issues, mythology for example. According to the myth, Zeus required Pegasus to bring him his thunder and lightning, a task the horse was able to accomplish. Are we to suppose that there is some specific way in which Pegasus managed this seeming impossibility—in its mouth, on its back? The world of Greek myth is full of magic and strange powers and forces. Accordingly, perhaps it is reasonable to claim that Pegasus did it in a certain way; indeed, we can imagine finding a myth dealing with this very matter. On the other hand, this judgment does not seem clearly right; it seems equally plausible to suppose that the laws of logic as well as those of physics are suspended here. Since there is no way of being sure that it is the laws of logic rather than those of physics that are being violated, it is hard to be confident that logical completeness fails in such genres as these.

Dreams, on the other hand, provide a remarkably divergent set of cases, and there are instances where it is reasonably clear that completeness fails. Let us consider more realistic varieties first. Although dreams differ widely in such factors as coherence, vividness, emotional content, color, and psychological time occupied, some are extremely lifelike. In fact, it is not uncommon to be unsure (for a brief time, anyway) whether events really happened or were dreamed. In such instances there seems no difficulty in invoking the principles of narrative fiction: there is a setting that is to fill in undreamed details, there is full continuity and coherence for the actors in the dream, and even logical completeness holds. Where a dream is about familiar people, earlier considerations about fictional writing concerning historical characters seem appropriate, as the dream figures are in an analogous way based on these real people although the dream is not directly about those people themselves. The distinction between what one does "in reality" and what is done in dreams is applicable; one's biography does not include dreamed events (whether in one's own or in others' dreams).

Dreams make one notable divergence from fiction: in the dream the dreamer usually has a part, participating both through actions and as a spectator. Is this the real person there? Consider a film shot from the perspective of one of its characters. Here a viewer puts himself into the depicted situation as one of its agents, performs the acts indicated, feels to the degree he becomes involved in the action the emotions appropriate to the character, and the like. To the extent that he is able to do this he becomes the character, it is natural to remark. Yet one would not say that the real person himself is in the movie, that it is about him as a historical individual. The facts about the character are very different from those about the real person. Even if amazingly the film events are just those of the real person's life, the film is about a created character and not about a real individual. For a viewer of film where the viewer plays the role of a character, a knowledge of his own actual historical status is always available even if he is not actively thinking this at a given moment. He watches this variety of film with a sort of double consciousness of himself as real person yet as presently adopting the role of an individual in the world of the movie. It is because of the technical possibility of photographing the action in a certain way, together with the psychological fact that a viewer can suspend knowledge of himself as a real person and temporarily assume the role of a participant in the film world, that there can be movies having the experiential perspective of ı ı lıuıuutuı. But such a film leaves intact the conceptual diotinctıous luılılıny for realıetıo oinema.

The same is true for dreamo, the differeuce being that in the dream one typically identifies strongly with the figure experiencing the events. In the dream I really do think of myself as fully being that person and have all his feelings and cmotions. In contrast to this, someone watching a film normally is aware of sitting in a theater watching a movie; this sense of self and the detachment it provides can always be recalled no matter how absorbed one becomes in the film. In a vivid, realistic dream I have no such sense of a detached self having a dream; my whole being is for the moment taken up with identifying with that dream figure. But I am that person only in the sense of being for that time psychologically identified with that figure, comparable to feeling momentarily one with some character in a novel or movie. That I do not realize that the qualification "this is in a dream" applies to my current experience does not mean that it does not apply. When I wake up—when I begin to experience myself as a real person having my familiar historical situation—and realize that what I had been living through is a dream, I unhesitatingly employ the full logical apparatus of the outside standpoint. I fully acknowledge that the dream figure was only my counterpart and that what happened to him in that particular dream world did not happen to me in the real one. These same distinctions apply to the phenomenon of lucid dreaming, where one can manipulate the contents of one's dreams. There the individual is operating with the consciousness that the present events are part of a dream world and not reality, and so one can attempt to affect them (apparently with success, for those who have mastered the technique) simply by willing changes. Here one is experiencing the dream with the realization that one is so doing; if one is a character in the dream one is playing a dream role with the awareness of being a real person playing a dream role. In fact, if one did not have this double consciousness at this point, one could not think of oneself as able to manipulate dream contents. As merely a dream character, and without the realization that I am a real person playing the role of a dream character, I do not have the thought that I can manipulate the dream simply by willing it. These considerations do not make it inappropriate to analyze dreams for interesting psychological content, for after all their author is my unconscious (or whatever theory one has). Still, when one believes that he has learned something in a dream about another person or himself, the conceptual structure is the same as that present in fiction "about real people." In such an instance, the dream figure is clearly drawn from real life and represents the individual; it is surely right to transfer what is exhibited in the dream to the actual person. But dreams are about real people only in the secondary sense that the dream figure is given the characteristics of the real person—in the way that historical fiction is based on real individuals and only indirectly about them.

Often dreams are fuzzy with objects only partially distinct and changing obscurely into others; there is frequently no clear sense of setting; background is indefinite or almost nonexistent; and logical principles are loose and vague. Normal logical regularities are simply not found in such dreams. G. E. Moore, a thinker who emphasized clarity and precision if ever anyone did, once reported a dream in which he could not distinguish a proposition from a table. If we suppose that there was some object in Moore's dream with regard to which he could not make this distinction, then this is a case where logical principles constituitive of the standard way of regarding reality are not in force. Moore's proposition-table is logically incoherent, since it has properties of things belonging to disparate conceptual types. Depending on the details of the dream, this object would be not incomplete but overcomplete, so to speak, having full complements of properties from two divergent conceptual ranges. Notice that it is still an object in the sense of this study, something to be talked about and discussed (we are discussing it now). Meinong might well include it as something to be investigated by the theory of objects. The literary analogue of Moore's dream would be a story about such an object. On the principles elaborated earlier, whether there could be such a thing would be a matter of whether its including story would be accepted in actual practice—as in the partly comparable instance of the tale of the round square. Fiction, and imaginative writing generally, usually requires more coherence than is found in dreams of this type, so it is perhaps doubtful that literary counterparts of Moore's dream would be generally acceptable. But the acceptability of a text as literature is not a matter of such a priori considerations as what logical principles it incorporates, so the philosophical analyst cannot make such pronouncements with confidence. In any case, generally speaking dreams are much less regular in the principles required for their interpretation than is fiction: dream reports do not have to conform to the purposes of such writing, and we should not be surprised to find there that, logically speaking, anything goes.

This is the place to comment on modernist writing, a genre one purpose of which is to react against realistic literature and to reject at least some of the conceptual regularities it embodies. A representative piece is the aforementioned *Six Characters in Search of an Author*, in which a rehearsal of one of Pirandello's own plays is interrupted by six characters who want to perform a different play for the other actors. As this latter production finally gets performed, it is ever more difficult to distinguish the play within the play from the play itself; indeed, *Six Characters* is one of a trilogy where conflicts between author, characters, and actor-manager are explored. A film that trades on similar themes is Woody Allen's *The Purple Rose of Cairo*, in which a character walks out of a movie to become the romantic interest of a member of the audience. Other cases are novels in which biography and creation merge (consider Proust's great work) or in which an author provides alternative endings between which the reader is to choose (John Fowles's *The French Lieutenant's Woman*). It is difficult to know how to analyze such works—a consequence no doubt intended by their authors. In the Pirandello, Proust, and Allen cases, it seems possible to make a reasonably firm distinction between the contents of the work and reality (i.e., our reality), for each of these pieces has a definite content given in the work itself. Fowles lets the reader create the fiction, as it were, partly taking over the role of author. Within the worlds of these creations, the inside/outside distinction is pointedly violated, this being central to the meaning of these works. Perhaps one might feel that despite these violations this distinction *must* hold in these works and that a careful examination would sort out the conceptual levels within the various pieces. This is doubtful; there seems no reason why these principles are inviolable, and given the license authors enjoy to introduce new forms of literature we should expect there to be works not adhering to traditional constraints. In this study I describe structures characteristic of realistic fiction; what other forms of imaginative writing there can be is a matter of what would be accepted by an appropriate audience. Modernist fiction questions these structures by making them its subject matter and radically manipulating them or even self-consciously violating them. Perhaps in some cases it employs different principles altogether. It is worth repeating, however, that such writing presupposes a grasp of ordinary fiction, since anyone who lacks this certainly has no understanding of the contents, much less the point, of Pirandello's play and Allen's movie. Modernist fiction may or may not adhere to the principles of realistic writing, but it certainly presupposes an understanding of them. It is not a

form of literature intelligible apart from the mainstream
Western literary tradition.

There are also forms of representation quite apart from
this tradition, and something should be said about them.
There is storytelling that requires audience participation by
chanting or dancing; dreams are sometimes considered experiences of alternate realities or messages from spirits or
from people physically dead but alive in some afterlife
state; automatic writing or trance speech can be conceived
as performed by real beings in a different dimension of reality. These conceptions might be integral parts of religious
cosmologies or conceptions of nature foreign to standard
Western thought and could be associated with such practices as group celebrations and festivals, forms of prophesy
or revelation, storytelling as part of the transmission of
tribal culture, certain forms of monastic instruction, or
shamanistic rites. From the Western perspective whose
principles I am describing, groups accepting these world-
views could be seen as failing to draw important distinctions between fiction or myth and history. But from their
own perspective these groups simply differently conceive
reality and its constituents and differently classify events
such as storytelling and dreams. These modes of thinking
and the activities connected with them might be entirely
unfamiliar to standard Western thought with its predomi-
nantly scientific worldview. It is worth remembering that
this conception has been in place for only a few hundred
years and that it has as one of its direct ancestors a worldview giving an important place to oracles, various forms of
augury including divination by dreams, and stories of gods
having transactions with mortals. The conceptual structures elucidated in this study would probably have some
place in these alternative ways of thinking—pure storytelling is, after all, one of the great pleasures of mankind—but
they might have a very different place and not be related to
what is conceived as reality in ways characteristic of con-

temporary Western culture. These alternative ways, and the various developments in recent Western art mentioned, suggest that many forms of imaginative thought are possible and that standard conceptual divisions may appear in surprising and unfamiliar kinds of logical relationship. The distinction between what is in the story or experience and what is in reality might be weakened or practically eliminated or applied quite differently, logical completeness might have no place or only a diminished one, indeed reality itself could be conceived differently with corresponding changes for criteria of the real. Presumably these modes of representation would be governed by conceptual principles that could be discovered by descriptive analysis of the type exhibited in this study; such structures would not lack logical regularities but would incorporate ones different from those presented here. The mind is extremely inventive and there are no limits to be set in advance on the conceptual structures it finds it natural to adopt.

7

IS EVERYTHING FICTITIOUS?

Is the everyday world fictitious? A typical philosopher's question—taken outside a philosophical context the answer is so obvious that the question itself can only seem frivolous. And from the perspective of this study there is certainly the assumption of a firm distinction between what exists and what is fictional; to allow that we are not sure how to apply it is to call the distinction itself into question and so make nonsense of the position I have been articulating. Nevertheless, it is interesting to entertain this question, which has, after all, been put forward by serious thinkers. Dealing with it calls for further elucidation of basic conceptions, which turn out to have unexpected and instructive applications. The question itself has somewhat different senses depending on who is asking it: the skeptic wonders whether I have any reason for thinking that I am not just a character in a vast cosmic story, the metaphysician suggests that everyday reality is less real than some further plane of being, and the moralist recommends that standard attitudes toward reality be abandoned in favor of superior ones. It is obvious that in taking on these issues we are leaving the rather localized logical problems generally associated (in Western philosophy) with the problem of nonbeing, for they require excursions into more speculative territory involving metaphysical and even ethical issues.

These issues—except for the skeptical one, which I believe can be given a decisive response—cannot be settled here or even discussed very fully; rather, I intend to show how the distinctions emerging from the preceding analysis can be used to illuminate these proposals in a novel way.

HOW DO I KNOW THAT I AM NOT A FICTIONAL CHARACTER?

The skeptical issue is nicely put by Parsons:

> Even if I don't doubt that I am something, how can I know, say, that I am not (merely) a (native) object of a very detailed and cleverly designed story? What can I learn about myself which would ensure my reality? I am human, male, brunette, etc., but none of that helps. I see people, talk to them, etc., but so did Sherlock Holmes.[1]

One possible response here is analogous to a reply often given to the suggestion that the world is the product of my dream. To describe reality as dreamed, "dreamed" must have a contrast with "not dreamed" or "real." But this contrast is ruled out by the world-is-my-dream suggestion according to which everything is included in my dream. This suggestion therefore makes false or meaningless the claim of dreaming. Similarly, for me to describe my world as "fictional," there must be a contrast with "nonfictional," a

---

1 Terence Parsons, *Nonexistent Objects* (New Haven, Conn.: Yale University Press, 1980), p. 218. A native object is one that originates in the story in question. Of the skeptical issue Parsons remarks, "It seems to me that this is a philosophical problem that deserves to be treated seriously on a par with issues like the reality of the external world and the existence of other minds. (I don't know how to solve it.)"; ibid., pp. 218–219. See also Robert Nozick, "Fiction," in *The Mind's Eye*, ed. Douglas R. Hofstader and Daniel C. Dennett (New York: Bantam Books, 1982), pp. 461–464.

contrast made impossible by the hypothesis that my world is entirely fictional. So the skeptic must face a dilemma: if "fictional" retains its normal contrast with "real," it is plainly false that the everyday world is a fiction; if it does not retain this contrast, the skeptic's question loses its intended sense. This reply seems perfectly adequate, but I want to offer considerations more closely related to the analysis of fiction presented here.

If I am a fictional character, then I am a grammatical object, merely something to be referred to and described and not having any form of existence. This is absurd; I am not something having this status. I exist; at least there is some level of genuine existence which I enjoy. Whatever this level should turn out to be, it is different from that which merely conceptual objects possess. Absolutely speaking, a fictional character does not have any reality whatever and so belongs to an entirely different category from me. The skeptic's response to this would no doubt be that perhaps I merely exist in the story in which by hypothesis I appear, for there I can be said to be real and to be contrasted with fictional characters that have merely conceptual status. This contrast can hold without making me actually real, since it obtains in the tale I inhabit and not in reality—and the skeptical possibility is maintained. This response ignores the chief point to be made here, that from the standpoint of my absolute conceptual classification I have genuine reality and am not a mere referent. It is not that in some story I have existence; it is rather that absolutely I exist—I exist simpliciter and independent of any descriptions true of me under the scope of some operator. It is conceptually absurd for me to think that I have the status of something that can merely be talked about, that I am just a grammatical object as absolutely speaking fictional characters are. It is true that there might be a story with a character who is six feet tall, a philosopher, who lives and teaches in such and such places, and who in the story is contrasted with characters in stories in that story. Yet when one asks what absolute classification such a character would have, the answer is that it is a grammatical object, created by an author's putting down certain sentences. Clearly this is not *my* absolute classification. I am a real person born to two parents and presently writing out a comment on a philosophical puzzle. If one asks how I know this, the reply is that I know this through the ways in which one does know such things, by living in the world, learning in obvious ways who I am and who my parents are, and having this knowledge reinforced countless times. But so did Sherlock Holmes, the skeptic replies. No: *in the story* it is true of Holmes that he learned such things. Given the story we can say that Holmes did this. We are licensed to say this of a character only given a story in which that character appears. What we are then speaking of is a grammatical object, something with no status in reality. But none of this is true of me; there is no story in which I appear in the way that Holmes does, and I am not merely grammatical. If there were a story about someone just like me, I would not be in that story in the way that my fictional counterpart is. To describe me as a fictional character would be to make a category mistake on the order of saying that the number seven is salty or that the direct object of a sentence owns a Volvo.

It is interesting to compare the possibility of dreaming with being a fictional character. Dreaming is an experience that practically everyone has. We know what it is like to fall asleep, dream, wake up, and recall the contents of the dream. But there is no sense to the idea of a real person's being a fictional character in the world of a work of fiction. There is no such thing as entering the world of the fiction, having experiences there, returning to the real world, and recalling the events of the fictional world. If we try to imagine such a thing happening, we imagine something falling under a different classification than becoming fictional. Suppose I try to imagine becoming a character in the Holmes stories. I imagine myself talking with Holmes and Watson, taking rooms with Mrs. Hudson at 221A Baker St., accompanying Holmes on adventures, and so on. There is no problem imagining this, but is what I am imagining my becoming a fictional character? I am imagining participating in certain events, but should they be described as "becoming a fictional character"? I could be describing a dream, but having a dream is not becoming a fictional character. I could be imagining having genuine historical experiences; possibly such events could really occur or have occurred in the past. What I am entertaining at this point are genuine historical possibilities, where Holmes, Watson, Mrs. Hudson, and all the rest are actual people really living in London during a certain period. This has not made me fictional but has changed literary characters into real ones—or, strictly, has provided historical counterparts for fictions. So, to try to imagine circumstances in which I enter a fictional world in the way that I can enter a dream situation results in nothing of the sort. Or put this in the third-person context. Suppose someone quite seriously says that she has actually become a fictional character and lived in the world of Sherlock Holmes for a while; she has "fictioned" this world, as she might have dreamed it. One would not know what to make of this: is it a joke? Is she actually describing a dream after all? Has she been hallucinating? Has she gone insane? Possibly she just does not understand the language and means something other than what her words convey. These are the possibilities we would look for, since her words do not describe any recognizable situation. The only way of encountering fictional characters is by reading or hearing about them; only in this way can one "enter a fictional world." This makes for an important distinction between the possibility of dreaming now and being in a fictional world now. There is sense to the former possibility because there is the experience of dreaming, waking up, realizing that one has been dreaming. But there is no sense to the suggestion of being in a fictional world now, coming out of it, and realizing that one has been "fictioning." For neither of these possibilities can the skeptic make a plausible case, but at least for the former one the case can get started because we know what it is like to be in the situation that generates the skeptical doubt. With the latter instance the skeptic does not have even this as a starting point. There is something it is like to be in a dream, but there is nothing it is like to be a fictional character.

EVERYTHING IS FICTIONAL: THE METAPHYSICAL THESIS

The metaphysical theory that the everyday world is fictional has been held by certain Buddhists, who "put all objects over which our thoughts and other psychological activities range at the same level"—that is, they hold that there are no fundamental distinctions between present, past, and future things, fictional and imaginary objects, and the logically impossible. The claim is that anything whatever is fictional; this has been called the "pan-fictional" view, and I adopt this terminology.[2] Pan-fictionalism taken literally cannot be correct, for everyday things are not items to be talked about only—as indicated in the previous section. Nevertheless, this proposal has an interest beyond the question of whether on a literal reading it is true. Probably the pan-fictionalist can best be understood as putting this idea somewhat misleadingly and intending to be making a proposal that can be more accurately couched in logical terms. This is, perhaps, that important aspects of the

2 Bimal K. Matilal, *Epistemology, Logic, and Grammar in Indian Philosophical Analysis* (The Hague: Mouton, 1971), pp. 145, 134.

logic of fiction apply to everyday reality even if ordinary things are not literally fictions. At any rate, this is the interpretation I develop (without trying to provide textual evidence for it).[3] Pan-fictionalism typically takes one of two forms. It holds that there is some higher reality to which the ordinary world is subordinate and which gives the claim of pan-fictionalism justification, or it holds that our beliefs about everyday reality result from an interpretation of some nonconceptual given. I call these two cosmological pan-fictionalism and interpretational pan-fictionalism. Before considering these positions, I have one further comment.

It is interesting that both forms of pan-fictionalism accept as sound the principles adopted in ordinary fiction. There is an opposition between pan-fictionalism and common thought, but this lies not in a straightforward rejection of everyday concepts and distinctions but in a different application of them. I might emphasize one particular theoretical commitment of pan-fictionalism. Since it accepts the correctness of the principles of common thought, and one of these principles is that common entities are logically complete, pan-fictionalism must hold that the fictional counterparts of ordinary things are logically complete. This is just the view presented in the preceding chapters; on this issue, pan-fictionalism is consistent with the analysis of fictional discourse given here.

In order to discuss cosmological pan-fictionalism, I must point out a logical feature of the fictional operator not so far noted. One of the properties of statements asserting the contents of a work of fiction is that they are governed by an operator of the form "in B, x is F" (or, "B says that x is F"), where B is the work and x a fictional entity. An implica-

3 There is further discussion of such matters and of other materials treated in this and the following section in my "Everyday Reality as Fiction: A Madhyamika Interpretation," *Journal of Indian Philosophy* 9 (1981):323–333.

tion of this schema is that B is real, or at least that it is real relative to x, which is merely an item in the fictional world that B sets out. To claim that the ordinary world is a fiction is to hold that there is something that has a greater degree of reality than the constituents of this world and which has produced them. I want to suggest that, despite its terminology, cosmological pan-fictionalism does not intend to imply the absurdity that the contents of ordinary reality are only grammatical objects. Instead it holds that everyday reality has a lesser degree of reality than the being that creates it; there are levels of reality, with the ordinary world genuinely real if less fully so than its creator. It is interesting to recall philosophical positions which (explicitly or implicitly) include an operator analogous to that governing fiction. On Berkeley's view, ordinary things are merely objects in God's mental life and hence our world is the product of God's thought. God's mental contents have the same conceptual structure as works of fiction, with a thinker who produces these contents where these are to be asserted under an operator ("God thinks that p," where p states some fact in the created world), and further God could be held to have a higher degree of reality than his creations. Here God's thought creates the ordinary world, which is not however unreal, if the earlier discussion of skepticism was correct, but real. Like the world of a dream it is entirely dependent on God's continuing to think it and thus to maintain its existence. God is the "author of our being" but unlike more ordinary authors gives genuine if dependent reality to his creations. Another metaphysical outlook that gives a secondary and dependent status to ordinary reality is nontheistic idealism, Advaita Vedanta, for example. In this outlook there is a self or consciousness, Brahman, which imagines (thinks, dreams) the phenomena we take for ordinary reality. A difference in degree of reality is clearly acknowledged by this theory in its characterization of ordinary reality as Maya, illusion. Yogacara Bud-

dhism has a similar conceptual structure, and Schopen
hauer and other German idealists are Western philosophers
with comparable views. Bradley explicitly acknowledged a
difference in levels of reality; for him the Absolute alone is
fully real, with the empirical world being so only to a lesser
degree.[4]

The second version of pan-fictionalism takes as a model
not the complex of author and created fictional world but
one of mistaken interpretation. On this conception something is given to thought or experience and is wrongly understood as something else. The world is like a coil of rope
taken to be a snake, as one of the stock illustrations in the
Indian philosophical tradition has it. Here an object created
by the interpretation—the snake—is plausibly regarded as
unreal, rather than as real (in at least some degree) as is the
coil of rope. The everyday world as commonly understood
is the product of an act of interpretation, with nonconcep-
tualized experience as what is given. On this conception
we ourselves are the creators; we impose the categories of
common thought on an objectless given, or at any rate on a
given that has features entirely different from those with
which we endow it, and thereby generate the contents of
the world in which we live. We are creators who live in the
fictional worlds of our own making, ourselves self-created
characters. On this outlook we are creators through interpreting given phenomena as constituting a set of objects
rather than through producing sets of characters and their
situations by writing about them. Plato held that, in the
cave, shadows were wrongly interpreted as reality and that
what was real were individual souls and, outside the cave,
the world of Forms. Hume can be read as holding that sen-

---

4 See F. H. Bradley, *Appearance and Reality: A Metaphysical Essay*
(London: Oxford University Press, 1951), especially chap. 24, "Degrees of
Truth and Reality."

sations are interpreted without justification as representing a real, external world. Kant and the German idealists immediately after him claimed that there is a preconceptual given on which the categories are imposed, resulting in a conceptual structure postulating the objects toward which our beliefs are directed. This act of interpretation-postulation does not result in illusion but in principles and objects necessarily adopted if there is to be any knowledge at all, at least on Kant's version.

These two variants, the creator and fictional world version, and the illusion version, could be combined by supposing that some creator or external source provides us a set of phenomena for interpretation, resulting in our perhaps necessary but still self-generated ordinary conceptions and the objects to which they apply. This would be double pan fictionalism, as it were, since there are now two authors: whatever produces the phenomena in the first place, and ourselves, the interpreters of this phenomena. There are two levels of object: the level corresponding to the phenomena produced, which is real although perhaps dependent and belonging to a lower level of reality, and the level corresponding to the objects believed to exist as the result of an interpretation being imposed on these phenomena. Plato seems to have held such a view: the demiurge creates the material situation that is wrongly interpreted by the inhabitants of the cave as constituting a real world. Perhaps this view can also be attributed to Advaita Vedanta and to Yogacara Buddhism and also to Schopenhauer and possibly other German idealists. Kant and Schopenhauer adopt a distinction that bears on this discussion—that between empirical realism and transcendental idealism. This distinction allows on the one hand for a realm of transcendental entities of a kind unfamiliar to everyday thought and on the other for possibly less real but still genuinely existing ordinary objects. These latter entities result from our interpretation of the phenomenal given and are guaran teed their reality by the conceptual requirements of our ba sic framework— as shown by a transcendental argument. We can see various thinkers filling in the details of such an account in various ways (consider the differences between Advaita Vedanta, Plato, Schelling, Fichte, Schopenhauer, and Bradley, for example). Kant, perhaps Wittgenstein, and most versions of Buddhism can be regarded as sympathetic to the possibility of a transcendental dimension of reality but remaining agnostic or skeptical about it. There are evi dently many possible positions given the different concep tual variables the logic of the situation admits. The enter prise of supporting any of these positions lies beyond my purposes; nevertheless, wherever one's sympathies lie, it is clear that a familiarity with the structure of ordinary fic tional discourse helps to clarify such views and is useful for evaluating them.

ETHICAL ATTITUDES TOWARD
REALITY AS A CONSTRUCT

Sometimes metaphysical pan-fictionalism is made the basis for recommending the adoption of an ethical attitude toward reality as a whole; I call this view ethical pan-fic tionalism. This outlook extends principles characteristic of fiction to everyday things in claiming that ordinary, com monsense objects have their properties merely conven tionally rather than through possessing metaphysical na tures reflected in ordinary attributions. This claim is backed by the recommendation that literal discourse be re garded as having many of the characteristics of fiction. Au thors write about purely grammatical objects that they themselves create. It is plain that the logical principles governing this writing could not possibly represent any meta-physical natures inherent in these objects, for it is obvious that they have none. Furthermore, authors, having decided to write fiction, have the choice of genre of fiction and thus the decision of which conceptual constraints to adopt. So the conventions applying to the fictional objects are in several ways functions of authors' choice rather than of the objects themselves. In holding that ordinary things are fictions, the pan-fictionalist means to imply that literal language shares important features with fictional discourse, especially that basic principles definitive of reality result from choice rather than reflect fundamental metaphysical facts. Ordinary things are more like fictional objects than we usually suppose. In particular, it follows from the conventional nature of everyday speech that the referents of ordinary language are not timeless metaphysical substances, the building blocks of the universe, but objects conveniently introduced for various practical purposes. Misled by the fact that language contains names for things, the metaphysician comes to believe that reality consists of eternal, unchanging entities. This mistake is a common one among philosophers and appears again and again in widely differing viewpoints. It has produced atomic particles, Platonic forms, Aristotelian primary substances (on one interepretation), Cartesian minds, Leibnizian monads, and phenomenalistic sense data, for example. These conceptions are highly specialized, but the nonphilosopher is not free of this substantializing tendency, particularly with regard to the idea of a self or soul, which has been conceived as something strictly self-identical and eternal. In calling everyday reality a fiction, the ethical pan-fictionalist draws attention to the conventional nature of the principles constituitive of common discourse, claiming that it follows from this that the objects referred to under adherence to these principles are nonsubstantial and noneternal.

A second aspect of fiction integral to the this outlook, one not emphasized in the preceding chapters, is brought out by focusing on the relation between a reader of a work of fiction and the fictional world appearing in the work. When one reads a story and learns its contents, one has become acquainted with a fictional world that can then be the subject of interest, concern, curiosity, emotional responses, and moral evaluations. It is a familiar fact that one can be deeply absorbed in a detective story, becoming extremely interested in what is going to happen next and wondering who the murderer is. In this state, we have to a fictional character the same sorts of emotional reactions as to a real person in comparable circumstances. The murderer, when he or she is finally found out, is judged to be as evil and as deserving of punishment as a real individual who has committed the same dastardly deed. Holmes's persistent search and clever solution elicits our admiration just as would similar achievements on the part of a real detective. We become concerned at a danger to which Holmes and Watson are about to be subjected, or intrigued with the possibility of Holmes's romantic affiliations (with Irene Adler in "A Scandal in Bohemia"?). There is, of course, the notable difference that a reader is removed from the narrated events. Though Holmes is injured in a story I am absorbed in, I do not begin to wonder how I can help or try to telephone Watson to find out how Holmes's recovery is proceeding. This removal does not result from some physical or temporal barrier, as if Holmes and Watson were in a distant city or had lived at a past time, but from the conceptual station fictional characters occupy. To attempt to make a telephone call to Watson, a character in a fictional work, is to act on an intention that includes a logical absurdity. This difference in conceptual levels is part of what is conveyed by the operator "in the story, p," and anyone understanding it realizes that the story is something real and that its content (i.e., what is asserted by p) is a set of fictional situations. Such situations do not have the conceptual standing that would make intending to interact with them logically coherent.

These considerations point up the fact that a knowledgeable reader of fiction has an attitude of detachment, in the sense above, toward the fictional world as a whole. It is not that only some particular item in the fictional situation receives this detached outlook, but that everything in that world does. Clearly one does not react to Holmes with appropriate conceptual distance but treat Watson as real. A fictional world is an entire set of characters, events, and background circumstances all bound together into a unity, and it is from this entire totality that the mature reader is conceptually removed. In calling everyday reality fictional, the pan-fictionalist is recommending that we take an analogous attitude toward the things in the real world. The way of thinking and reacting we normally take to real things, being one of active involvement, is quite different from that we take toward fictions. Our normal attitude regards our immediate environment as a place where one has an existential relation to many different kinds of thing and may act in different ways toward them, and where there is perhaps an inclination to act unreflectingly and possibly egoistically on one's immediate emotions, wants, and desires. To recommend regarding the world as a fiction acknowledges the existence of this naturalistic attitude, as it might be called, but it also calls attention to the possibility of adopting a different stance, one comparable to that which we take toward a fictional world. In construing ordinary reality as a field for potential activity, one has taken it in just one of various logically possible ways.

The pan-fictionalist is suggesting that this attitude of involvement is not inevitable and should in certain respects be replaced by that of detachment—particularly where egolotic matters are concerned.' It is partly for this reason that the Buddhists mentioned above have recommended looking at the world as a fiction, it is fundamental in their view that one should overcome egoistic reactions of attachment to possessions and matters of personal well-being. Complete detachment is not intended, for ordinary reality would then become a place conceptually inappropriate for action; the intentions basic to ordinary life would then be logically out of place. In particular, it is part of the Buddhist outlook that one must survive practically and develop certain virtues (compassion, patience, diligence), partly in order to help others achieve this same attitude. Pan-fictionalism serves a heuristic function for these Buddhists in that it recalls a context that illustrates at least some of the principles Buddhism encourages. Thus it helps to give sense to its recommendation of changing reactions of possessiveness and self-centeredness and the like for a more reflective and compassionate attitude. In partial support of this recommendation, the pan-fictionalist can appeal to the logical principle of conventionality.

5 An anonymous reader imagined a different reaction to viewing the world as fictional—one of great personal responsibility and ethical anguish, a la Sartre, rather than one of detachment. Presumably one would not feel responsibility for the world in exactly the way that a writer might feel responsibility for his or her literary creations. Probably Buddhism conceives the world as created more in a social and linguistic rather than individual sense: society has adopted a set of social and linguistic conventions providing the objects available for discussion and giving them implicit values. Nevertheless, this reader's remark points up the possibility of different attitudes on viewing the world as a whole, including one of deep anguish and responsibility. Many issues are raised at this point; in "Serenity," *Journal of Indian Philosophy* 12 (1984):201–214, I discuss the general notion of an attitude toward the world as a whole and also the particular attitude of serenity. According to the Buddhists recommending it, this attitude is the one appropriately accompanying the kind of detachment discussed above. This attitude is not, I think, incompatible with a commitment to social change (see "Serenity," pp. 208–209). Above I am merely presenting *one* position incorporating a world-as-fictional theme.

At this point the theses of the conventionality of ordinary things and of the possibility of a different attitude toward them can be combined into a unified general view. If everyday objects are conventionally constituted in the sense indicated, and particularly if there is no eternal, self-identical soul, then at least some philosophical objections to the Buddhist's ethical recommendations are undercut. It cannot be argued now, for instance, that each of us is essentially a substantial mind or eternal soul to which we owe primary allegiance. A non-egoistical attitude toward life is taken to be supported by pan-fictionalism's claims of the nonsubstantiality of the constituents of the everyday world.

This discussion has gone rather rapidly through heavy conceptual terrain, and it may be useful to point out the concepts essential to ethical pan-fictionalism which have counterparts in ordinary fiction. The idea of *the world as a totality* that one confronts and is conceptually outside, the notion of an *attitude* toward this world as a whole, the implication that one such attitude is the familiar *naturalistic stance* including a self-centered perspective, the suggestion that there are *alternative attitudes* and especially one including, at least in some measure, the *detachment* illustrated in our standard reaction to the contents of a work of fiction—these are notions integral to ethical pan-fictionalism which its suggestion of regarding everyday reality as fiction helps to illuminate. It also makes the further claim that from the plausible thesis that language has a conventional basis one can infer that everyday objects are not metaphysical substances and hence that the the appropriate attitude toward reality as a whole includes some measure of detachment. I have much sympathy with this position but am not trying to justify it here; I have merely pointed out the role that concepts counterpart to ones constituitive of our understanding of fiction have in this position. At least this seems clear: ethical pan-fictionalism is compatible with the notion that concepts for ordinary things occupy a central place in our framework. That a set of objects is conceptually basic has no bearing on what attitude it is appropriate to take toward them. There is, I think, much more to say about ethical pan-fictionalism, but this is not the place to say it.[6]

6 Among contemporary Western philosophers, Wittgenstein and, I believe, Heidegger seem to have most in common with the outlook suggested here. In the last pages of Tractatus Logico-Philosophicus, Wittgenstein uses some of the concepts discussed above (the notion of being confronted with the world as a whole and the suggestion that there are different attitudes that might be taken toward it), and his later view of language as consisting of a complex of language games serving various purposes seems compatible with some of the claims of conventionality found in ethical pan-fictionalism. I discuss Wittgenstein with some of these concerns in mind in "The Suchness of Things: In Buddhism, American Transcendentalism, and Ordinary Language Philosophy," Zen in American Life and Letters, ed. Robert S. Ellwood (Malibu, Calif.: Undena Publications, 1987), pp. 51–66. For helpful exposition of Heidegger, see Michael E. Zimmerman, Eclipse of the Self: The Development of Heidegger's Concept of Authenticity (Athens, Ohio: Ohio University Press, 1981).

INDEX

Absolute classification of objects.
See Objects: absolute
Advaita Vedanta, 165, 167–168
Anscombe, G. E. M.
  direct objects and existence, 64–
    65, 102
  intentional vs. material objects,
    53–55
Aristotle, 40
Attitudes toward the world as a
    whole, 171–174
  anguish, 172
  detachment, 171–173
  naturalistic, 171–173
  serenity, 172

Baker, G. P., 19
Being. *See* Subsistence
Berkeley, George, 165
Bradley, F. H., 166, 168
Brentano, Franz, 3–4, 9, 22, 30
Brody, Baruch A., 42
Buddhism, 163, 165–167, 172–174

Carnap, Rudolph, 122–124
Castañeda, Hector-Neri, 17
Chisholm, Roderick M., 4–5, 9

Dennett, Daniel C., 159
Descriptive approach to nonbeing,
    18–21, 59, 112, 122–124, 156–
    157
  Meinong's views and, 76–77
  relation to formal semantics,
    20–21

relation to philosophical ther-
    apy, 18–20
Descriptive metaphysics. *See* De-
    scriptive approach to non-
    being; Strawson, P. F.
Donnellan, Keith S., 33–34, 55
Dreams, 150–154, 161–163

Edwards, Paul, 4
Ellwood, Robert S., 174
Evans, Gareth, 36, 46, 48–52, 66,
    72

Fichte, J. G., 168
Fictional discourse
  as adopted, 59–61
  as originating in storytelling,
    80–90
Fictional operator, 23–26, 28–30,
    94–95, 97, 108–110, 134, 140
  implies conceptual detachment,
    170–171
  implies levels of reality, 164–
    165
Fictions
  as a conceptual type, 59–63
  as created, 61, 65–68, 90–91,
    100
  as unreal, 62, 64–72, 97–98,
    103–105
Films, 144–145, 151–152, 154–155
Findlay, J. N., 5
Flew, Antony, 26
Frege, Gottlob, 28

Library of Congress Cataloging-in-Publication Data

Crittenden, Charles, 1933–
    Unreality / Charles Crittenden.
      p. cm.
    Includes index.
    ISBN 0-8014-2520-4 (alk. paper). —ISBN 0-8014-9754-X (pbk.:
alk. paper)
    1. Fiction—20th century—History and criticism. 2. Nonexistent
objects (Philosophy) in literature. I. Title.
PN3331.C75 1991
809.3′19384′0904—dc20   90-55739